More Books From 1

Miss Havilland: A Novel by Gay Daly

The Orphan's Daughter: A Novel by Jan Cherubin

Lifeboat No. 8: Surviving the Titanic by Elizabeth Kaye

Into the River of Angels: A Novel by George R. Wolfe

Who She Was: My Search for My Mother's Life
by Samuel G. Freedman

The Stories We Tell: Classic True Tales
by America's Greatest Women Journalists

New Stories We Tell: True Tales by America's New
Generation of Great Women Journalists

Newswomen: Twenty-five Years of Front-Page Journalism

The Someone You're Not: True Stories of Sports, Celebrity,
Politics & Pornography by Mike Sager

What Makes Sammy Jr. Run?: Classic Celebrity Journalism Volume 1 (1960s
and 1970s) edited by Alex Belth

Our Washington, DC: America's Hometown in Transition
edited by Susan Sheehan

The Dreyfus Collection: A Novel by Estelle Rubin Brager

See our entire library at TheSagerGroup.net

Thinking of You

A Memoir of a Girl's Crush, a Teacher's Grooming, a Forbidden Love and the Journey to Reclaim My Voice

MARY BETH RUNNOE

Thinking of You: A Memoir of a Girl's Crush, a Teacher's Grooming, a Forbidden Love and the Journey to Reclaim My Voice

© 2025 Mary Beth Runnoe

Cover design and interior design by Siori Kitajima, PatternBased.com

Cataloging-in-Publication data for this book is available from the Library of Congress.

ISBN-13:
eBook: 978-1-958861-70-7
Paperback: 978-1-958861-71-4
Hardcover: 978-1-958861-72-1

Published by The Sager Group LLC
(TheSagerGroup.net)

Thinking of You

A Memoir of a Girl's Crush,
a Teacher's Grooming, a
Forbidden Love and the
Journey to Reclaim My Voice

MARY BETH RUNNOE

THE SAGER GROUP

Artifex Te Adiuva

Contents

Author's Note

Dear Reader,

Thank you for engaging with my story. Before you read, I find it important to supply a trigger warning for those who need it. This book contains mentions of grooming and predatory behavior that resulted in the emotional manipulation of a teenager.

I used to believe in right and wrong. I found solace in the idea that good and evil were separated by a harsh, unyielding line. Perhaps it was the perfectionist in me, forever drawn to the idea of a script for an outstanding performance, or as a way to protect myself from the threats of evil. Whatever the reason, I stifled my own healing with this belief.

Over the past decade, I have tried and failed to fit this story into several boxes categorized as abuse, regret, and trauma, none of which saved room for my feelings of gratitude for the mentorship and support in our relationship. Through my attempts I have learned to accept the presence of many truths, coexisting in the space between.

While I recognize that there is a clear antagonist in my story, it is not my intent to label him as such. The consequences have felt disproportionate, but I believe there is freedom in releasing the need to level the scales. For me, justice is a quiet peace. It is for this reason that I have chosen to share this story in anonymity. All names of characters, excluding my own, have been changed. Nevertheless, the story within remains based on my lived truth, and details are gathered from my own memories and feelings, alongside the artifacts left with me.

This story is mine to share, and in doing so, I hope we can make progress together, whether through connection or conversation, though I do hope for both. I wish to use my voice to inspire conversation about appropriate behaviors, emotional boundaries, and potential red flags to watch for in an effort to protect our youth. It is my belief that stories are meant to be shared, and so I am giving mine to you.

With love,
Mary Beth

Acknowledgements

Hannah, thank you for reading my tarot cards and pressing into this story. You set fire to my gentleness exactly when I needed it, and you continue to feed the flames. You are my best friend.

Alana, this book was quite literally your idea. I am grateful for your beautiful mind. Thank you for editing, drawing out metaphors, and celebrating every single win with a toast.

Erin, thank you for being my cheerleader and protector through this process. You never let me make a move without checking on my mind and my heart. You are the friend we all need but many do not find. I am lucky.

A special thanks to my love, let's call him *my* William. You were the first to hear this story in the aftermath and the very first to ever identify it for what it was. Thank you for promising me a lifetime of listening.

Thank you to everyone who listened. If I tried to name you all, I would have another book. Thank you for inspiring me, reading my entries, editing my grammar, and encouraging me to continue when I was ready to quit. I love you all, endlessly.

Prologue

"Mary Beth"

Dear . . .You,

    This letter is both overdue and overthought. So much so that I was not sure how to address you. William? Mr. Davis? Mr. William Davis? None seem to fit our relationship. I have fantasized about a confrontation with you since the last moment we spoke. Over the last ten years, I have wished to see you again, if only to make you face me. I have written countless letters that were never sent. As I reread my unsent letters, I can't help but notice the way my feelings toward you have vacillated but never settled. The themes have ranged from grief to rage to indifference and back again in a relentless, exhausting cycle.

    I have been angry with you, but the rage always slips away too quickly. Everyone else in my life seems to find that this emotion comes easily when I tell them about you. Sometimes, if I try, I can conjure resentment for you. Unfortunately for me, I am quick to excuse your transgressions as a collection of tiny accidents, made in your darkest moments. These transgressions have left me with only a memory of someone who may have been either a broken, reckless man or a calculating predator. Neither choice allows me to remember you as the exceptional mentor and good friend I believed you to be. I should resent you for the loss of these once-golden memories, though the urge to mourn is stronger.

    I often wonder if you have been able to wash your hands and move along, feeling clean and free from guilt. After all, we haven't spoken in a decade. Did you ever experience remorse, or were you able to shift the blame from yourself? Have you ever told anyone about us or do you keep our history as your own dirty secret? Do

I stand in your life as a cautionary tale, reminding you to keep the boundaries that might prevent repeated history, or do you truly see no wrongdoing? I know it should not matter to me, but I cannot help but wonder. After all, your feelings on the matter may be able to help me determine whether you are worthy of my forgiveness.

What I can say about my own feelings is that, even though my anger is fleeting, my disappointment is persistent. No matter your intentions, you let me down. If you read this book and see a girl with an unhealthy obsession, well, you would be both entirely correct and fully wrong. I have been unhealthy and obsessed, but I no longer blame myself for this.

I wish I could forget you, but I cannot. Unfortunately, your memory is tied to a million little things I would not wish to forget. The sounds of music that I once performed now force me to recall the time spent with you in rehearsals. Remembering the biggest accomplishments of my teenage years cannot be done without accepting the hand you had in my success. Forgetting you is not a viable option for me because your influence runs deep into the depths of a formative and vulnerable time in my life.

In order to move on, I have tried to divide you into two individuals. In one version you are my beloved teacher. You are a man who taught, challenged, and supported me as I grew up. The other version is a man who used my religion and his power to fill his own needs without regard for the consequences. It's tricky to maintain this divide because the distinction between the two is unclear. As I look into our past, I wish I could bring the line into focus. I wish it were simple and that you had only ever been my teacher or that you had only been a source of pain. The coexistence of good and bad was incredibly confusing for the girl I was at nineteen. She couldn't see what I do now; that you were just one sad man. Our relationship was always unfair, and I was always the naive child.

I fear that this story means very little to you now. After all, the power balance was tilted in your favor. The consequences of your actions have stayed quiet, held down by the weight of power. However, I do not have the luxury of silence. The consequences of your actions have echoed throughout my life. If you listen closely, maybe you can hear them ringing through your own life. I used to think that sending a letter of my own might help you understand. I hoped that you would consider taking the chance to see the story from my perspective. I hoped that you might read my side of the story one day. I hoped that when you did, you could see the wreckage you left behind.

I want to believe that you know better. I want to believe that, at the very least, you won't do it again. I want to believe that you would not encourage this behavior from your peers. I want to believe that if your daughter found herself in my shoes, you would understand the hazards at play. I still want to believe that if you listen to me, you will. However, my thoughts of you are overly generous.

Thinking of you,

Mary Beth

1
Memory

"I start this way to say . . ."

Memory is admittedly an unreliable source. At best, we may remember the approximate truth. At worst, the human brain has been known to create false memories, the roots of which from any form of reality. Most likely, our memories are generalized versions of our story with some variance in the details that is not plot-altering.

As a true crime enthusiast (a character trait you are free to analyze on your own time), I have listened to many cases that have hinged on memory as key evidence. In the unfortunate case where the victim is not available, a case may hinge on the testimony of eyewitnesses. I am always fascinated by the variability in the details given by a group of individuals who supposedly witnessed the same event. The car may have been red, or was it blue? The driver? He may have been wearing a hat, or he may have been a woman with hair flowing past her shoulders. Memory does not often misremember, but instead fills in gaps for us to create a congruent story. Those details, such as the color of the car and the gender of its driver, were seemingly unimportant, so they were not stored. Instead, the brain fills those gaps without altering the story. Because of the fallibility of memory when it comes to these details, eyewitness testimony is considered important, but not conclusive.

In the case of a survivor, this memory comes from the victims themselves. Forcing victims to recall their stories in a room of strangers who are there to determine whether they are to be believed has always felt like yet another abuse against them. However, the truth is that memory is often more reliable when recounting a trauma. Our brains are hardwired to lock in and fixate on the details that would otherwise have been forgotten. Therefore, a victim's testimony is a powerful thing.

In this case, I am not just an eyewitness. I am the key witness. I am the victim. And while misremembering details and jumbling timelines is quite common, the complete fabrication of a memory is unlikely. I once worried that the combination of time and trauma may have warped my memory in such a way that I could no longer be a reliable narrator for my own story. I thought perhaps I misremembered your advances or at least that I had embellished the favor you showed me. Luckily (or unluckily, for you), you left me with physical evidence.

While I have always had one artifact from our relationship to bolster my memory, I was constantly seeking more. As I did this, I recalled the way our relationship developed over the exchange of texts and emails. Because I am a millennial, I have been taught from a young age that a digital footprint is forever. I became determined to find yours. I searched the cloud, dug through my social media messages, and tried to break into old email accounts. I did so until I felt crazy and a bit obsessive. I refuse to claim either label, but I will accept that I am persistent. On a whim, I made a phone call to the IT department at my alma mater. The kind voice on the phone assured me that nothing was lost, and in moments I had finally received access to a college email account that I had not opened in years.

I typed in "William Davis" and anxiously bit at my thumb as I waited for the emails to populate. I knew you had emailed me a few times, but nothing could have prepared me for what I would feel reading your messages again as a grown woman. Instead of finding that I had imagined our relationship to be something it wasn't, I found that I had majorly downplayed your manipulation and blatant abuse of power. I discovered pages of notes, devotionals, and what can best be described as Christian essays from you. There were attachments that opened to recordings of songs written and performed by you, which I have not been able to sit through to date. I had not anticipated the physical reaction I had to opening these attachments. The flood of memories and repressed feelings made me physically ill at first. It took several breaks, a glass of wine, and the presence of supportive friends to make it through the files and emails. Once I had, the memories I have of you were recategorized.

Through the reformation of my memories, the light, vibrant color of my time as your student has dulled. Instead, my history is painted in a sad and confusing palette of gray. In what I know was an attempt to protect myself, my mind had ignored minor details of my memories. I had added nuance where there was none and watered down your pursuit of me in order to preserve your memory as my favorite teacher. Even with the physical proof, I have had to make a conscious effort to accept the new perspective on my past.

And so, this is me accepting my story as it is, with every messy, inconsistent twist. I am committed to writing it down in truth and to recounting every piece to the best of my human mind's ability. It will not be perfect, and the eyewitnesses may offer critiques. Nonetheless, I am the only one I trust to tell my story.

2
The Very Beginning

"I can't wait to see what God has in store for you, me, and us."

Fifth Grade

I grew up in a small town, each grade level contained only 100–120 students, at most. Because of this, it was not uncommon to be remembered. Many of my teachers could recall my older brothers by name, and my classmates became a sort of dysfunctional family over the twelve years we spent together. I grew alongside the same group of peers from kindergarten to graduation, give or take a few. Throughout elementary school, we explored interests and settled into cliques within our grade levels. Sometimes, a rare opportunity to do so outside of the pocket we knew so well would present itself. This is how I met *you*.

When I was ten, the high school theater department was seeking children to play orphans for their production of *Annie*. The invite to audition was put out to girls in grades four through six and announced during our elementary music class. I remember the thrill of hearing about the opportunity with my friends. We kicked our little feet and giggled at the thought of sharing a stage with high schoolers.

I came from a particularly musical family. I had been reading music for years and was quite good at the piano, thanks to years of lessons. I had taken dance classes and loved attending our church's choir practice with my dad, who enjoys singing as much as I do. To say I was excited to share this opportunity with my parents would be an understatement. As I had expected, I was immediately met with support and encouraged to sign up for auditions.

A week later, the initial buzz had worn down. While originally it seemed that everyone I knew would audition, the list dwindled as the other girls felt the nerves or lost the desire to participate. In the end, we were left with eighty-six girls, which admittedly is still a lot, especially considering that only eight of us would be cast. I was incredibly intimidated, as one would expect, but as determined as always to stand out.

Because we were so young, one day of music class had been set aside so that we could be taught the audition materials. Those who didn't plan to audition were expected to participate and would consider it their regular music class. We were handed the materials for auditions, which included a form and a short excerpt of the sheet music from "It's the Hard-Knock Life."

Our teacher, whose name I do not remember, stood to address the room, with the signature five claps. The crowd fell silent, or as silent as a group of excited preteens can be. Once she had our attention, her face relaxed into her warmest smile. "We have a very special guest today. While I could teach you this song myself, we thought it would be best that you learn and get comfortable singing with the music director himself. Everyone, say hello to Mr. Davis, the high school choir director and music director for *Annie*."

She gestured to the door, and you entered with the confidence of someone who is beloved by all. You stood tall and confident. Your dark hair hung in thick waves down to your chin and you had a full beard. In hindsight, the overgrown aesthetic made you appear older, even though you were only twenty-four at the time. Then again, what do I know? I was only ten.

It was actually unremarkable, meeting you this way. The only reason I remember it now is because I wanted to impress you for the sake of the show. I wanted you to leave remembering my face, so that I might make it onto the cast list later. I belted my little heart out as we learned the song, and I introduced myself on the way out, thanking you for your time. I am sure you smiled, and I am sure I smiled back, but I really don't remember.

Auditions came and went, and within days my mom received a call from the directory saying I had been cast as Duffy and asking if I would accept. Because I had the bedtime of an elementary-school child, my dad woke me up from sleep to congratulate me. I think this is the first time I experienced true pride in myself. Whether I was cast because of my springy curls and round face, my projection and portrayed confidence, or my impressive singing didn't matter so much at ten. I had never felt such a sense of accomplishment in my young life. Funny how such a huge milestone for me is now indisputable evidence of the disparity between us. Perhaps fourteen years felt small to you when I was nineteen. Then again, perhaps it didn't. For me, it feels monstrous when I think of you seeing me at ten with my Limited Too shirt with the little monkey on it and my hair pulled into butterfly clips.

Sixth Grade

The next year, in sixth grade, every student was required to take a music course. We were given three choices. We could enroll in either band or choir, or we could split our time between the two. I, along with most of my peers, chose both. On Tuesdays and Thursdays, I came to your class. I think I enjoyed it, but it was largely forgettable. I retained very little about this time and decided my energy was better spent elsewhere, because I dropped choir again the moment it was no longer required in seventh grade, and I did not opt to put it back on my schedule in eighth grade.

Eighth Grade

Then, in the second semester of my eighth-grade year, another opportunity presented itself. This time, eighth graders received an invitation to audition for the high school musical. This was a common practice that continued through my senior year. As a small school, it was a successful method used to bolster the ensemble and spark interest for students heading into high school. It certainly worked, as many of us went on to form the core group of "theater kids" in high school.

I auditioned for this show in a room with you and the stage director, Mr. Hamilton. I sang "Gotta Find You" from *Camp Rock*, which happened to be the only musical I cared about at the time. With clammy hands and a shaky voice, I stumbled my way through my audition. My voice had cracked and I flubbed an entrance, but I was overall proud of my attempt.

When I finished, you congratulated me on having the courage to show up and asked why I was not in your class. I explained that with only one slot for extracurriculars in my schedule, and as an aspiring teacher myself, I had chosen to be a teacher's aide. You leaned back in that casual, cool way of yours and shook your head disapprovingly. "If you are serious about performing, you really ought to be in my choir, Mary Beth." You gave me a wink when I told you I would definitely make room in my schedule next year. I thanked you for your time and ran to the hallway to let out my post-audition nerves with my friends.

Over the course of rehearsals for this show, I got to know you a little more. I learned a lot from you and enjoyed every bit of your goofy, creative personality. As far as I could tell, I didn't catch your attention in this show. I received none of your favor, which was seemingly nonexistent. I cannot recall any student who received the attention that I would when I came through your program. Our lead was not a choir student, and you spent most of your time joking with the boys. Then again, I didn't know you like I do now. It's hard to remember what I thought of you before you became such an influence in my life.

In this time before high school, I noticed you in the way I noticed the rest of my teachers. In hindsight, it was nice. It was simple. It feels silly to begin our story this way, with such ordinary, mundane events; however, it's the truth. I was too young to notice you the way I did in high school, and you had not yet noticed my potential. This story begins with a teacher and his student. It is an uncomplicated and painless beginning to a story that is so difficult to tell. Regardless, it is important because so often, these stories begin in normalcy.

3

On My Own (Part 1)

"Though you couldn't see, a tear came into my eye."

Ninth Grade

My freshman year in high school I was still incredibly timid about singing. I had come a long way in a few short months since I joined choir, but I wanted to be better. Like the first tastes of something decadent and sweet, the more I sang, the more I craved. One day at school, you mentioned that you offered private vocal lessons. The second I got home, I begged my parents to let me take lessons with you. Their rebuttal was an offer to continue to fund my private piano lessons or to switch and pay for vocal lessons with you. The choice was one of the easiest I ever made. I knew I had found my instrument.

You taught me a lot over that year of lessons. You taught me how to breathe while I lay across the risers: "Now, put your hands on your belly. Good. Breathe deeply and feel how they remain steady." I closed my eyes and tried not to worry about whether you could see my belly expanding. You called me out on this though, apparently you saw my attempt to hide my stomach. You had me stand and watch myself in the mirror at the back of your room. I was self-conscious of my body and hesitated to watch my own reflection. You promised that bellies should expand when we breathe. I believed you and let this comfort me.

One day, I left my rain jacket in your room. You ran to catch me before I left the building, shouting, "Here! Sorry, I just don't like to have female students' things left in my room. You know how it looks. Anyway, have a good night!"

When I had a fight with a friend or a boy hurt my feelings, you listened. We talked about my problems and you offered reasonable solutions, always reminding me that high school is not forever. It was good advice.

Through my private lessons with you, I gained some confidence. One night at my voice lesson, you encouraged me to take the chance on a principal role in the spring musical, which was to be *Les Misérables.* Considering you were the vocal director for the show, I trusted your judgment, though I was new to the world of theater. The expanse of my knowledge was a straight line going from *The Phantom of the Opera* to *The Sound of Music.* Being the teacher you were, you took my lack of knowledge as a challenge. You showed me clips from your favorite shows, and we discussed the characteristics of a good audition song at length (i.e., range, tone, style, character). It was during one of these discussions that you asked if I had ever heard of the show that I was getting ready to audition for.

"I haven't," I admitted.

You stood, walked across the room to your desk, and retrieved your laptop as you spoke. "Oh, the music is lovely and tragic. I think it suits you." You opened a tab and started typing. "Oh, let's see." You scrolled through videos until you reached one titled, *Lea Salonga—"On My Own,"* which of course is one of the most memorable songs in *Les Mis.*

You pressed play and took a step back, leaving me alone. I took in the dramatic instrumentals, wondering what scene would unfold before me and why you had made this choice for me. The music changed suddenly, filling the room with a sweeping, romantic melody. A young woman stepped into the light. She was tragically beautiful, as you said. Like me, she had dark curls, though hers had been tucked into a cap. Windblown whisps hung across her forehead. Her face was flushed, rosy cheeks peeking through the smears of mud and dirt. When she started to sing, I was captivated. She was a contradiction there, alone on the giant stage. The richness of her voice was in juxtaposition with the poverty in her appearance. She was wrapped in a trench coat and stood braced for the cold, yet her tone was filled with warmth. She appeared young, perhaps a teen like me, yet her eyes showed the depths of a life much heavier than mine. The devastating beauty of the poetry in the lyrics transported me to another, very sad world. By the time the song stopped, I was entranced.

We sat in silence for a moment as I grounded myself back to reality.

Finally, you took a step closer, placing yourself next to me as you shut the computer. "Well? What did you think?"

"I think I need to watch that musical," I said, my voice dripping with awe.

In the following months I fell, spinning, into a rabbit hole. I watched the twenty-fifth anniversary production, which to my absolute delight featured Nick Jonas. My teenage heartthrob aside, the one who stole my heart was in the 2012 movie version of *Le Mis*—Samantha Barks in the role of Eponine. To this day I will tell anyone who asks that she was the greatest.

I auditioned with sixty seconds of "On My Own" that had been selected and perfected in my lessons with you. When the cast list was posted, I read my name next to my first principal role. I was at once excited and terrified. I ran, shaking, to your room. "Oh my God, Mr. Davis! Oh my God!"

You smiled at my reaction. Of course you already knew the cast you had selected. "You did that, MB. Congratulations."

"On My Own" became my lucky song and *Les Miserables* became my obsession. One that not only remained through years but grew as I matured to understand the depth of the characters and their story. This was the beginning of what would become a lifelong love . . . that is, until it hurt to recall the origin of that love.

4

Haunted

"I think of you daily."

As far as I think I have come, the consequences of your decisions ring through my subconscious and echo in my dreams as my mind tries to process our relationship. I have burned sage, diffused lavender, and attempted everything short of dark magic to make these dreams stop.

Unfortunately, the haunting continues to this day. I keep a journal in my nightstand. When I wake, I scribble the dream as if to purge the poison of your imagined presence. I hope that by transferring the visions onto the pages, they will find a new residence there. But like the prodigal son you claimed to be, they always come back.

Because I have to live with this vivid, unrelenting loop, so will you.

5

Invisible

"I want more time to see you this time."

I sit in your classroom. It still looks the same, but I do not. My curls have fallen into soft, dark waves, and though I still have bangs, they are parted in the center. My body shows the curves of womanhood in my straight leg jeans. Though I am fully a woman, I sit on the risers of your classroom, one leg curled up between my seat and me. I am excited to be participating in a reunion of sorts with my high school peers. We are buzzing with excitement to sing together once more when someone says, "They brought Mr. Davis back too!" My stomach drops and I become aware of the way I am spiraling into a panic attack. I cannot breathe. I am desperate for air that does not come. I stand, struck by a need to escape before you arrive. Instead of stumbling through the exit, I stumble directly into you. I look up, expecting you to be as shocked as I am that we are in the same room again. Instead, something strange happens. You don't notice. You straighten and walk away, as if I were an inanimate obstruction that you are moving past. Somehow it hurts even more. I follow you, hoping you might notice me after all. I am forced to consider that you do notice and this is your choosing to ignore me. Your eyes never pass me as we rehearse. I try desperately to get you to laugh with me again or to compliment my vocal growth, but you are determined to deny my existence. I think you may be angry with me, perhaps because I declined a relationship with you. I *am filled with regret and longing to take it all back. What was once my favorite part of every day has become my personal hell.*

I awaken in tears and spend my day wondering what you think of me now.

6

Young Love

"I know you struggle with your image issues and how others view you."

Ninth Grade

My freshman year of high school, I started to notice boys. They had been noticing me for years, and I had always played along for the attention of it all. I had my first kiss at a pool party in sixth grade with a boy I had barely spoken to at the time. He told everyone he liked me for my "great boobs," and I liked that someone was talking about me at all. Every "boyfriend" since was a status symbol or strategic move to fit in with my peers. They asked, I said yes; we called each other boyfriend and girlfriend but never once called each other just to talk. After a couple of weeks, one of us would tell a friend to send a breakup note, and we'd move to our next "relationship." Generally I found the boys my age to be gross, uninteresting, and mean.

That is, until I fell for a senior boy named Aaron. He was tall and a little bit awkward, which I found endearing. He was also incredibly talented and deeply in touch with his feelings. Our paths first crossed during rehearsals when I was cast in the high school musical the previous year. Upon my transition into high school, Aaron noticed me. He was all about me and I was smitten. He left sweet poems in my locker and texted long notes that made me feel beautiful. Funny how I cannot recall those words after all these years, yet yours swirl in my mind, untouched by time. He learned about my musical interests so that he could sing my favorite songs for me, and after school we would walk and window-shop our way through our small, antique town. Our whole relationship was a whirlwind of teenage love and sneaking into corners of the school for time alone together.

One winter day, we sat together on an empty stage between school and rehearsal. He was playing his own version of "Chasing Cars," while I rested my head on his shoulder with my eyes closed, trying my best to commit the moment to memory. The bench was small and our legs brushed each other's, causing innocent little butterflies to flutter in my stomach. He had such a beautiful voice, and I was taken by the romance of it all. When I was fourteen, being serenaded on an empty stage by a talented eighteen-year-old boy with skinny jeans and long hair was a dream come true. When he finished singing we sat there in silence, letting the last note ring into the atmosphere. I turned to face him, only to find that he was already looking at me. He reached down and caressed my cheek, pressing his forehead to mine.

"Hey . . . I like you," he whispered. I didn't say it back. I was feeling a little dazed in his presence. I wasn't sure I even possessed the ability to speak, so I just smiled up at him.

We shared a sweet kiss there on the dark stage. It was teenage bliss, until I heard footsteps. I jolted away from Aaron, nearly falling from the bench. I found myself standing and jumped an extra foot away for good measure.

"Hey now, you two . . . " you said, with a tone of disapproval. You were clearly aware of what we were up to moments before.

My stomach sank as I realized we had been caught. "We were just practicing!" I said, through panic, hoping you might believe me.

Aaron laughed, closing the gap between us as he grabbed my hand. "Sure, that's what we were doing," he said with the confidence of an eighteen-year-old boy.

That evening at vocal rehearsal, I could barely look at you. I was so ashamed for not only being caught breaking the rules, but for being caught kissing a boy at school. It was a teenage Mary Beth's actual nightmare, and I felt a deep urge to make it appear less damning.

It was dark by the time we finished rehearsing, but I lingered as you packed your things.

"I'm sorry about that," I said, "It wasn't my fault, we were just playing piano and then he . . . " I stopped and buried my face in my hands, too embarrassed to continue.

"I don't blame you," you said gently. "Just, be careful, okay? He's quite a bit older, you know. I don't want to see him take advantage of that."

I blushed and fumbled my way into the first lie I ever told you. "Oh I know. It's kinda weird, isn't it? He's like obsessed with me. I don't even like him, I swear."

From that moment on, you referred to Aaron by several names including "cradle robber" and "creeper." You maintained this position when he took me to prom, doubling down on the creepiness of the whole relationship. When my peers would start to tease me, you were quick to join in on the fun. I was a good sport, laughing alongside you at Aaron's fascination with someone so much younger. Funny, isn't it?

What I never told you, or anyone, is that with every jab from you, I pulled further away from him. When he whispered in my ear that he loved me while we danced at prom, I didn't say it back. In fact, I felt so uncomfortable about it that I told him if he wanted to love me he would have to do so in secret. When he begged me to stay with him while he was away at college, I declined, saying a college student couldn't possibly have anything in common with a high schooler. I told him our lives could not work together when he was taking on adult responsibilities and I was making my way through high school.

Eventually, the relationship fizzled, unable to withstand the pressure of hiding away from everyone so that they wouldn't see us together. I did my best to forget it even happened. Every now and then, you would remind me about the time I was caught kissing a boy four years older than me and I would blush and laugh like it was just so silly.

I cannot say that I love the idea of an eighteen-year-old senior boy pursuing a fourteen-year old freshman girl. I just find it funny that you had such a strong opinion on the matter.

7
Crush

"The first spark in my mind and heart . . ."

Tenth Grade

Y ou were a handsome man in your late twenties, and I am here to tell you that the girls in your class noticed. I am certain that I am not alone in my feelings on this because we talked about it. We talked about you. Gushed is the more proper term, really. My own crush started alongside my peers. At lunch, we obsessed over your dark hair and the way it was set carefully in perfect swoops. Our male counterparts were boys who couldn't grow facial hair, but you were a grown man with a trimmed beard and hair on your chest that would sometimes peek through when you dressed in your casual Friday V-necks, which we giggled about when you turned away. Collectively, we swooned over your voice and the way your bony fingers moved over the keys of the piano so gracefully.

However, my crush started to feel a bit different than my peers'. I noticed this when it grew beyond your physical appearance and into a gooey feeling I got when you laughed. I started to feel a buzz through my veins when you gave me one of your signature smiles that made your eyes crinkle in the corners. I found my breath turned heavy when you sang a part in the choir or at rehearsal, and it left my body completely when you winked at me. When I tried to relate to my peers about these feelings, they laughed at me and called me obsessed. I wish I could say that deterred me, but I never related to my peers enough to value their opinions on the matter.

My junior year I dated a boy named Zeke. It was a true show-mance that began when we were cast as love interests in the school musical, *Once On This Island*. It stayed in a state of mild infatuation until he dumped me in the choir room one night after rehearsal. Zeke was a cute boy with long blondish hair, and I liked the way he made me laugh, but he was not gentle. During one of our dress rehearsals for the show, Zeke was absent. I was relieved at first. After all, singing love songs on stage with my ex-boyfriend wasn't particularly enjoyable. It was a sacrifice I made for the sake of the art. Anyway, because the rehearsal was so important, worry sparked over our ability to rehearse without our male lead.

You and I had spent a significant amount of time together. I was in choir, musicals, and the a cappella group you had created. I suspect this is why you felt the need to approach me before we were called to our places for the top of the show. I was standing in the wings, sipping my warm water with honey, and reviewing my lines when you came up from behind and whispered a soft, "Hey, MB. Question for you."

I startled and my water spilled on the front of my costume. Embarrassed, I put my water on the props table and scanned the room for something to dry my costume.

You laughed. "Sorry, kid. I didn't know you were mid-sip, shoot."

"Oh no biggie, I just get antsy before a performance. It's fine though; it's just honey water." I laughed when you passed me the handkerchief from your pocket. "Thank you . . . but oh my God, you're like my dad."

You rolled your eyes at that as I blotted the small stain on my chest. "I was thinking, if I read and sing for Zeke, would it help? With your rehearsal, I mean. I know how hard it is when no one is singing or acting with you."

I froze in that moment, recalling the touchy dancing and lengthy stage kiss in my blocking. I think you saw the shock on my face even in the darkness because you continued quickly, "Not on stage, no no! I will sit in the audience. Are you comfortable with that? I can have a kid read if you want."

"No, that's fine!" My words came out a bit more shouty than I had intended. I was flustered by your offer. I knew in my head it was simply a reasonable solution, but a small part of me hoped you had wanted to sing with me. I was fully delusional, but silly little crushes will do that to a girl. I handed you the now-damp handkerchief. "Sorry, I hope it isn't all sticky."

"That's on me. I should know better than to sneak up on an actor backstage," you said, as you stuffed the cloth in your pocket. You ran a hand through your hair as you turned away, leaving it pleasantly tousled and leaving me flustered.

I found myself in full costume and makeup, on a stage, doing my best to act with the phantom voice coming from the house of the auditorium. When your voice came in for the big "love duet" of the show, I felt as if I would melt right into the stage. I stared at the empty space in front of me and imagined you there with me instead of hidden away in the shadows. Our voices rang out together in the weaving harmonies Zeke could never quite get right, and I finally found myself relating to my character's feelings toward the man who sang to her. What started as an effort to maintain my ability to act through the show, turned into a dangerous fantasy. When it came time for the stage kiss I blushed and bit into my lip, even though I was alone on stage. My castmates giggled in the wings, and I was so flustered I forgot the rest of my lines. In these pivotal moments of dreaming, my crush moved into something more like a fantasy where I imagined what it would have been like to know you in a world where we were equals.

I found the thought fascinating and allowed myself to entertain the ones that followed. In my wondering I realized I related to you more than I related to the kids in my class. Your humor, your interests, your dedication to your passions, all of you. I noticed the way you engaged in serious conversations with me and stayed late after rehearsal to discuss our favorite songs from *The Phantom of the Opera* or to show me a clip of an a cappella group that had moved you to tears. We bonded over a million tiny things, and for this I used to be grateful.

My crush on you was like the initial sparks of a fire, tiny embers glowing but not yet sustainable on their own. The fire was delicate and may have died naturally, extinguished by the elements of circumstance. Perhaps the flames would have retreated into darkness, unable to find the kindling needed to grow. Unfortunately, that was not the case. Instead of letting it die a natural death, you fed the flames until you felt the warmth of their glow. Eventually, I think you came to crave that warmth. I suspect this is why you stole it.

8
Seeking

"You are seeking, you are hungry for the Lord. That is beauty."

College—Year Two

When I went to college, I was desperate to finally fit in with my peers. I desired a place to belong and found this in an evangelical church on campus. The illusion of community they sold was a powerful one. I had spent most of my life learning about the Bible, but this new church told me it wasn't enough. Apparently, my previous acceptance of Jesus had been what they referred to as "lukewarm." Apparently I was expected to be "on fire." While some may have noticed the red flags and walked away, I saw yet another opportunity to become the best. I threw myself into studying their teachings, rededicated my life to Jesus (whatever that means), and accepted their rules for my body and my life. I impressed the staff members with my dedication to their God and was eventually accepted to join the leadership team. My need to impress the authorities in my life was extreme and unhealthy. I see that now.

By the time I was a sophomore in college, I had learned to evaluate my relationships, my success, and my value by the words of a man named Damien. Damien was a thirty-year-old former college athlete with charisma and a superiority complex who had climbed his way to the lead pastor position at the campus church. Damien taught us that in order to remain pure, dating must follow very strict guidelines. I learned that boundaries were key to success and was instructed to draw the line at kissing a boy, and even that was to be done with caution and without lust. Unfortunately for me, these teachings were yet another obsession. I became a part of accountability groups and began to focus on my sanctification.

As a woman on this journey, I was constantly enveloped in the shame of singleness and was desperately trying to find a "man of God" to save me. Believe it or not, these men of God were a rarity on a college campus. Every man—if we can call eighteen-to-twenty-one-year-olds that—who paraded himself as such was arrogant and insufferable. Nevertheless, I was told over and over again that I needed to find this elusive man to lead my future family and me. All of this was to be done while remaining cloaked in purity and righteousness. The responsibility for this was set on women because we were believed to be the only ones capable of holding physical boundaries in place. After all, women were not considered to be inherently sexual beings. I could say more on this, but I will spare you my ramblings.

The first time I thought I had found this man was in the summer of 2015. His name was Tony, and we met at a house party when I was home for the summer. My friend Ashley had found his group of friends and brought me along for this event. This was my first house party, and I used the excuse to wear my new daisy print crop top and tastefully distressed jean shorts. As the devoted Christian that I was, I was not yet willing to have a drink underage. Instead, I sat by the fire sober, watching the crew make drunken fools out of themselves. That's where I met him. He was sitting around the fire, keeping a watchful eye on his friends. He was the most handsome boy I had ever seen. He had dark curls that hung down his forehead, bronzed skin, and deep brown eyes. We chatted and I found out that he was also sober and a leader in the local campus church. He was a few years older than I was and I was immediately drawn to him. That summer turned into romantic nights exploring our local parks in the dark, kissing during the town fireworks, and laughing around a campfire with friends. I really liked him and thought we could make it something real before I went back to college. Instead, he broke up with me over a chai tea latte at Panera. He said he needed to focus on his ministry, and I was an unnecessary distraction. His parting wisdom to me was a recommendation to avoid wearing crop tops. He said that if I wanted to attract a guy like him in the future, I might try dressing the part. I dropped my daisy shirt off at Goodwill, determined to do better.

When I returned to school for my sophomore year, I was broken-hearted and my confidence had taken a pretty big hit. There was a boy I had gotten to know my freshman year named Jackson. Jackson was smart, handsome, and a bit of a dork. He was also capable of being one of the meanest guys I knew. What he called "brutal honesty" was actually an excuse to bully girls into thinking he was too good for them. My freshman year he told me I was a solid seven out of ten. In hindsight I should consider myself lucky; he told a floormate of mine she was a four. When I scolded him for this later he shrugged and said, "she asked."

I crushed on Jackson, hard, all through my freshman year. We had lunch together with my roommate daily and eventually I made my feelings known. He shot me down, but always kept me close enough to keep my hope alive. My sophomore year, I found out that he was a resident advisor on my floor, which meant he was responsible for creating community and keeping peace among his residents. At first I avoided him, knowing I was fragile and could not stand his rejection again. Then, slowly, we started to spend time together. He would walk me to hockey games, refusing to let me walk alone through campus. We would get lunch together at the dining hall. We made snow angels on our night walks through campus and eventually, we would spend late nights snuggled up on his bed, usually watching *Pirates of the Caribbean* or *The Lord of the Rings*. He taught me how to play chess and I taught him how to share his opinions with kindness. Our relationship progressed naturally, from innocent kisses to exploratory nights spent testing each another's physical limits. By winter of that year, we were a couple in every unofficial way. I started to see a future with him. It felt really special to be the one he chose, considering how many girls I knew had faced his rejections. He was still arrogant, but his iciness had started to thaw and he was kind to me.

When I confided my relationship with Jackson to my friend from church, things went south, fast. Instead of hearing that I had found a boy I liked who liked me back, she heard that I was kissing in a bed with a boy who was "barely Catholic." She scolded me and said that we were not "equally yoked." The next day, I was invited to sit down with a staff member who then removed me from leadership. I was told I was not in a position to mentor underclassmen because I could not remain pure myself. Apparently I had been unwise, sinful, and impure in my pursuit of Jackson.

During this conversation, I was told that I could make my way back into leadership with counseling from the staff and a few changes in my life. I was told that I could not possibly follow Jesus with a boy who did not put Jesus first for me. I was again told to look for a man of God who could lead me toward righteousness, and I was thus advised to break up with Jackson.

One night in early December, Jackson and I walked hand in hand. With each step I felt myself slowing, delaying the inevitable. We approached my favorite building on campus. Jackson looked at me, silently asking if I wanted to go inside. I nodded slowly, as the thought of what I had to do next elicited a burning sensation behind my eyes.

The little chapel stood in what was known as "old campus." The door was always unlocked as an open invite for students to enjoy the space. It was small, old, and filled with the charm of its history. There was a piano at the front and only about ten rows of pews. Red carpet covered the floor and windows stretched along the side walls. Some nights, when it was late enough for students to be tucked away in their dorms, I would sneak into the empty building to play the piano and sing. Jackson held the door open and placed a gentle hand on my back, guiding me inside. We slid into a pew at the back of the chapel. He put his arm me and I tucked myself into his chest. We sat in silence while I worked up the courage to speak. Finally, after several long minutes, I cried as I told Jackson about the pressures from my church. I told him I liked him a lot and was honest about my desires to stay with him. He comforted me and suggested that maybe I could leave the church because they treated me so poorly. I did consider it, but the moment was brief. I was in too deep. I told him we had to stop seeing each other. It hurt, but I was convinced it was the path of righteousness that I was so desperate to find. He held me and stroked my cheek as I broke up with him because he wasn't the man I needed him to be. I pleaded with him to remain my friend but he shook his head. He kissed me one last time and asked me to do him the kindness of never speaking to him again, which I have done to this day.

In a lot of ways, my life is a story of me putting the approval of others above everything, including my own happiness. I can see that theme as I put my memories down on these pages. I am sad for the girl who made every decision in the name of righteousness. Perfectionism stunted her growth and limited her story. She was never the author, but instead lived the paths laid for her by the expectations of others. And so I author her story and hope it may serve as a point of connection for others who find their own histories sharing these themes. If nothing else, perhaps her story can stand as a cautionary tale to illuminate the delicacy of power and the effects of its influence.

9

On My Own (Part 2)

"I believe your real beauty is inside and it shines through to the outside."

Eleventh Grade

In the fall of my junior year in high school, I attended a weekend honor choir event at your alma mater. This was an annual event attended only by those students who had been handpicked by their directors. I had the fortune of being chosen by you all four years. It always felt really special to attend an event where I was directed by a group of individuals who had once directed you. Little did I know, you had worked to make this year extra special for me.

The week before this event, you called our group of attendees up to the piano after class to collect our music. We always reviewed our parts together in preparation for the weekend. When we had determined a time for our next rehearsal, you dismissed the others. As I slid the music into my folder on the ledge of the piano, you tapped my hand softly.

"Hey, hang back a sec, would ya?" you said, low enough that the others wouldn't hear.

I nodded, anxious to hear what the others couldn't. Once everyone had left, you smiled excitedly. "I have a surprise for you."

"Oh?" I asked.

"I reached out to the faculty at the college and was able to schedule a private voice lesson for you during the event this weekend." You beamed. I could see the pride in your eyes, and it made me feel terribly important.

"Oh my God, you did? Wow. That's . . . terrifying." My initial excitement settled into nerves at the realization that this meant I would have to sing for not only someone new, but a faculty member at a university.

You sensed my hesitation. "It's a networking opportunity for you. Show her what you've got, and I will work on introducing you to the other faculty while we are there. All she needs from you is for you to prepare a song and provide the sheet music."

You had gone to some length to hatch this plan for me and I was flattered. You had shared a vision that I would excel in a collegiate program to become a music director, just like you. More so, you believed you had the resources to secure a position for me in this program at your alma mater, which felt oddly intimate. I wasn't sold on the stability of this path for my future, but I agreed to follow your lead regardless.

"What should I sing?" I mentally scanned my repertoire.

"I think you already know." You gave me a wink, and I couldn't help but smile. You always could anticipate my next move.

The day of this lesson, I showed up in a pink dress with my curls pulled into a loose bun. You introduced me to the white-haired faculty member, whose name I cannot recall. Then, you slipped out the door with a quick nod of encouragement.

"Alright, what have you prepared for us to work on today?" The woman asked, walking over to the piano and taking a seat on the bench.

I reached into my bag and pulled out my leather folder. I carefully tugged the sheet music from its spot (all six pages) and passed them to her. "'On My Own' from the musical *Les Misérables*."

"Wonderful choice," she said. *Les Mis* was and still is a classic among those invested in the musical arts.

She began playing the iconic entrance and like an automatic switch, I began to sing. I had practiced this song so many times, it flowed from me naturally. When I had finished, she walked me through a few of the notes and gave me some helpful tips about melding my upper and lower registers. As I prepared to leave, she said something unexpected.

"That was lovely. You have a beautiful tone, dear. But have you ever considered that you are more of an ingenue than an Eponine vocally? Maybe you should try a Cosette song instead."

I think she meant this as a compliment, or at least she was offering constructive feedback to guide me vocally. She wasn't wrong, either. I know that now. However, at the time, I was devastated. I had developed a deep connection with this sixteen-year-old character named Eponine. Her desire for a relationship that circumstance would never allow resonated in my bones. It didn't feel like such a stretch from my own reality. She was intelligent but had been forced into maturity much too soon. And like me, she was a dreamer who always left one foot in reality.

I remember coming into the hallway to fill you in on this development. "She said I'm more of a Cosette because I am an ingenue," I said, with a furrowed brow.

"Vocally, she's right." You shrugged.

"You think so too?" I asked. Disappointment filled my body at the thought. "What does that word mean anyway, ingenue?"

"An ingenue is an innocent young woman," you clarified. "Think Disney Princess. Are you not a Disney Princess?" You smirked and my mood lightened a little.

"I mean, yeah, I guess. But Cosette is so young and foolish. Eponine is smart and scrappy. Plus, her songs are better!" I argued.

"Just because your voice is pretty and sweet like an ingenue, doesn't mean you are young and foolish. Regardless, singing Eponine will make you a more well-rounded vocalist and performer. Keep singing what you love." You gave me a light nudge and changed the subject. "Let's get over to the auditorium for the group rehearsal, shall we?"

Over the next year, I became determined to prove that I was more than an ingenue. I worked on my belt range and dialed down my vibrato. I am not sure whether you noticed all of my efforts, but you certainly knew how much it meant to me.

Once again, I recall a story about the exceptional teacher that you were. You noticed my potential and you worked to ensure I had opportunities that were not so easily accessible for someone is such a small school. On its own, this is not such a terrible thing. Sometimes, I can convince myself that none of it was. Yet, as I place them together within their new context, these golden moments take on a darker hue. I wonder what it means now. Were your intentions that of an innocent teacher, whose only crime was recognizing the potential in his students, or was it just the ingenue that you noticed?

10

Rumors

"We can only control what we can control and that's not others, especially not their thoughts."

I n my four years singing in your choir and performing in your shows, I was never denied the part or solo for which I auditioned. Whether or not you intended, my endless success isolated me from my peers. While I continued to feel more entitled and confident, my peers started to see me as a "teacher's pet" or your favorite.

I am not sure if teachers are aware of rumors that spread among their students. In my years in the position of teacher, I have been privy to several, but I am not naive enough to think that I heard them all. Even as a student, I was only partially aware of the rumors that were being spread about you and me, about us.

Ninth Grade

I am certain you don't remember the evening the band was particularly loud during my voice lesson. I was exceptionally nervous to be attempting my upper range. (I was always terrified of making mistakes in front of you.) You misread my anxiety, believing it to be targeted at the fact that my peers were eavesdropping in the hall.

"I don't normally do this, in fact, I try not to . . . but I think I have to close the door," you said, as you slid out from your spot behind the piano. We finished my voice lesson behind that closed door. Obviously nothing untoward happened, but the students in the hallway noticed nonetheless. The next day at school, several students approached me and said, "I saw you and Davis had the door closed" in a tone best described as so high school.

"The band was really loud!" I replied, a little too defensive. I had thought nothing of it at the time, but now I was starting to hope my peers were right, that maybe you just wanted to be alone with me. That was the first time I became aware of what they said about us, but it wasn't the last.

I lived with the teasing every day. Secretly, I loved it. I knew in my mind that you were a happily-married grown man and I was your teenage student, but I started to want to believe them when they said you liked me . . . like, really liked me.

Twelfth Grade

It wasn't always welcome, though. I struggled with the paradox of wanting you to like me and needing to know I deserved every solo. My senior year you held auditions for a solo that would be performed at our competition in the winter. I auditioned, along with nearly half of the other girls in our choir. The next day, you posted the results. I approached the list with a group of nervous girls, pretending to share their uncertainty. We all read the note at the same time. The solo was mine. I turned and locked eyes with you across the room, a shy smile on my face as you gave me a wink.

"Thank you," I mouthed, as I put my folder away and made my way out of the room.

Later that day, I was headed back to your class for music history with a group of my friends. My best friend, Maverick, and I walked hand in hand, singing to one another in Spanish and giggling. From behind us, I could hear my friend, Deliah, loudly complaining. "Of course she got the freaking solo, and she's not even a soprano!"

I cringed as Maverick leaned into my shoulder. "Ignore her," he whispered.

"I can't," I whispered back, as I turned. "Stop it," I said, calmly, hoping that she would realize I had heard and apologize.

Deliah laughed. "Stop what? I'm just telling the truth. We all knew you would get it anyway. You're so far up Davis's ass, how could he deny you? It's gross."

I was filled with rage. I was beyond angry that she would not only devalue my own efforts to earn that solo, but to implicate you as someone who manipulated and played favorites. I had never been one to stand up for myself, but before I could think straight I heard myself snap. "No! You do this every single time you don't get something that you want and I am sick of it! Accept that I got the solo fair and square and move on!"

She recoiled, and I was suddenly aware that I had just screamed at someone in the middle of the hallway. Deliah ran ahead of us and ducked into the bathroom while Maverick pulled me into the choir room. I was shaking with adrenaline and was nauseated by an immediate wave of guilt.

"Oh my God," I whispered to Maverick.

"Girl, she deserved it," he proclaimed loudly, as he pulled me along.

You immediately picked up on my anxiety the moment we entered the room and left your stack of papers to come closer to us. "What's going on?" you asked, your eyes scanning me to ensure I wasn't actually sick, though I am sure I looked it.

"She just yelled at Deliah." Maverick laughed. "Don't worry, she was being a whiny bitch," he said, as if cursing in front of his teacher was nothing.

"I'm going to choose to pretend you didn't say that," you said, edging past Maverick and approaching me. "You need to talk?" you asked, your voice low.

"I'm okay," my own voice was small. I felt myself shrinking and wishing I could fade into the walls to avoid the consequences of my actions.

You looked up and immediately grabbed my arm and pulled me aside, out of the view of the door.

"Why don't you head to the bathroom until you feel steady? Take as long as you need." You were whispering, your eyes darting to the door as Deliah walked into the room.

I walked out of the room and into the bathroom, reeling from the interaction. I didn't realize I had let myself start crying. I splashed some cold water on my eyes, hoping the puffiness would go down quickly. Why was I so upset? Was it just that I wasn't used to the rush of yelling at someone, or was it bigger than that? I took a few deep breaths and shoved down all of the thoughts, telling myself it didn't matter what people thought, that I deserved your attention, just like I deserved the solo.

When I returned, you were teaching the class about some classical composer I couldn't be bothered to remember. Like most of my peers, I had no interest in music history. I only took this class to be near you. I took my seat and tried to breathe.

My mind was racing, wondering if you noticed the way they talked about us. Surely you weren't aware, or you would have tried to intervene by now. I was so scared you would get in trouble if anyone started to believe you had singled me out and showed me special interest. I felt responsible and wished I knew how to make them stop.

After class, I gathered my things and prepared to leave with Maverick. You stopped us at the door. "Go ahead, Mav, I want to talk to Mary Beth," you said. "I'll see you in a bit for rehearsal."

I panicked as l realized rehearsal would begin in fifteen short minutes. "I'm okay," I lied. I wasn't ready to face my peers again. I couldn't be sure Deliah was the only one feeling this way. I felt the tears start again, threatening to give me away.

You gave me that look, the one I knew well. Sometimes it felt like you saw right through me. In hindsight, I realize my emotions clung tightly to my sleeves and you were simply an adult who took the time to read them, unlike my teenage friends. "Follow me," you said, your voice low as students started to fill the hall.

I followed you through the crowded hallway and nearly lost you when you turned into a door I had never used before. I hesitated, unsure if I was meant to follow until I saw you wave me inside. On the other side of the door, I found myself in the teacher's lounge. All of the teachers were packing up in their classrooms, ready to leave for the day, so we were alone.

"Now, tell me what happened," you said, crossing your arms. "Was she giving you a hard time about the solo? I already spoke to her after choir and thought we had cleared that up."

"Oh God, what did she say to you? I'm sorry. I'm so sorry, I shouldn't have yelled at her, but she was whining about me getting the solo again and it really got on my nerves."

"Hey," you said, your tone filled with concern, "it's not your fault. I told her what I will tell you: You outperformed her. It's her responsibility to get over that, not yours."

At that moment I think you may have hugged me. At least, I wanted it so badly that I don't trust my memory assuring me it happened. Either way, your presence was a caress and I felt myself relax into that feeling of safety. You always had my back.

As you turned to lead me back to your room for rehearsal, you paused. "They're jealous of you and that's on them. I won't apologize for giving you the solos you deserve, and I need you to promise me to stop apologizing for being talented, okay?"

I nodded and stood straight, filled with pride knowing you thought so highly of me.

Unfortunately, that wasn't the last time the rumors made their way to my ears and the teasing didn't end, even when I graduated.

Adulthood

When I was in my twenties, I rarely found myself face to face with anyone I knew from high school. When I did, we would start reminiscing about high school and someone would always ask, "What's Davis up to?" They had no idea about us, but they had assumed I would have stayed in touch. I never corrected them because they weren't wrong, not entirely. I received several comments ranging from "you two were always close" to "I swear he had a thing for you."

The most disturbing came from a fellow choir member. She was an underclassman and spent two years with a different director after you left. We were talking and reminiscing about her early years in high school when she surprised me by saying, "Oh my God, Mary Beth, didn't you know what everyone said about you guys?" My palms started to sweat. *Did she know? Did everyone somehow know?*

"No, what?" I asked, refusing to give up our history that easily.

"Wow. I can't believe you never heard, everyone was saying it! Everyone said you were the reason he got a divorce . . . because you two were hooking up. Literally all of us thought it was true. Rumor was that's why he moved to Portland when you graduated. To hide."

"Oh my God, that's crazy," I said, feigning shock. While it should have made me upset, I found her story validating.

You once told me that you never saw me as more than a student. You promised me that you were not capable of such a thing. I wanted to believe you then, but I do not believe you now. I do not think I was crazy for feeling that this all started earlier than you promised me.

11

Face to Face

"Maybe some time to experience face to face interaction. What a novel concept?!"

College—Year Two

It was an unseasonably warm day for February. I sat on a bench in Old Campus. It was my favorite little corner of our campus. The buildings that stood here were the original buildings of the college when it was founded in 1910. The courtyard remained untouched, with stretches of green grass, tall trees, and winding paths. The campus chapel stood on one end, my dorm on the other.

I was sitting with my legs stretched across the bench, reading another book you had sent me. We had been texting back and forth all day, you between your classes and me during mine. My phone buzzed in my lap.

Driving home now, you free to talk?

I smiled and typed a reply.

Sure! Call whenever. I'm just reading that book you sent me. SO good btw :)

A message like this from my peers would have sent me into a spiral, worrying about what could possibly warrant a phone call. But not with you. You loved to talk on the phone and always made a point to call me at least once a day when you could. We would talk for hours every time. I looked forward to that time "together."

I answered on the first ring. "Hi."

"Hey, you. It's good to hear your voice. Today was a long one."

"Tell me about it, then." I curled my knees to my chest and set my book facedown on the bench, giving you my full attention.

You sighed. "Honestly, teenage drama is just silly. I had to diffuse what I think was quickly becoming a very public breakup in the middle of choir today."

"Ouch. Been there," I said, biting back my laughter.

"What? Surely, that's not true—I would have noticed!" you exclaimed.

"Well, it wasn't exactly public, but I was dumped in the choir room." I fiddled with a loose string on my sweater as I recalled that day sophomore year. I always felt nervous to bring up our past, as if it may cause you to realize what we used to be. As if you weren't already aware.

"Ahhhh," I could hear the realization as you put the pieces together. "Zeke?"

"Yup. He asked me to stay after rehearsal just so he could tell me I wasn't 'Christian enough' for him. It could've been a text, honestly." I rolled my eyes at the memory.

"That's so very . . . high school." You laughed. "For the record, you should have dumped him long before that. That boy was never good enough for you."

I was thankful for the distance so you couldn't see me blush. "Yeah, well . . . actually I don't really know why I held on for so long."

"What about you, how was your day?" you asked, changing the subject.

"Oh good. It's like fifty-five degrees here today, so I have been lounging around and reading outside."

"Ah, I wish I was there. Wouldn't it be nice, just to sit and read together?"

"It would be really nice," I agreed.

"I wish I could be closer to you. I want to see you . . . " you trailed off.

"Me too." I watched as the wind picked up, turning the leaves. I shivered at the chill of it, but refused to move from my spot. I wasn't ready to walk away from this moment with you, just in case you chose to finish that sentence.

"Hey, maybe we just have to get creative. I can't take you out to dinner like I want, but we could try something else?" You paused as an idea came to you, then continued. "It's not ideal, but I could FaceTime you. We could dress up, make a drink, and spend time seeing each other's faces, even if it is only through a screen. What do you say? Will you go on a date with me? More or less."

"I would love that." I felt the smile spread across my face and wished you could see it. I knew you wanted to give me more than this, but I was grateful for every bit of you that I did get.

We scheduled our date and laid out the plans.

On the day of our date, my roommate, Kristy, helped me prepare. She curled my hair and we sang along to the *High School Musical* soundtrack. She asked how I felt about a date with my former teacher and I told her I was excited. Kristy was a warm light in my life, and if I was happy she never questioned my choices. This was a rarity among my friends at the time.

Kristy made arrangements to be away for the evening so that I could have the room to myself. I set up my computer and adjusted the desk lamp to the most flattering angle I could find. The moment the call connected, I felt inexplicably tense.

"Wow. It's good to see your face," you said.

"You too." I smiled. Even though you seemed genuinely happy to see me, it did little to calm my nerves.

You held up a small glass filled with an amber liquid. "I poured myself some whiskey. I hope that's okay."

I nodded. "Of course it's okay. You're a grown man." I cringed. Why would I say something that called attention to the disparity in our circumstance?

"I'm a little nervous," you admitted. "I know we have been talking for a while now, but, well, it's a first date of sorts. First dates are scary."

I took a deep breath, hoping to open the tightness in my chest. I wasn't sure how to respond to that, so I agreed, "Yeah, they are."

We chatted for a bit about classes and teaching. You gave me a tour of your home and I showed you all 150 square feet of my dorm room. After an hour or so of this your tone shifted into something familiar, almost like the tone I remembered you used to speak to us about music theory in your classroom. It was controlled, almost scripted, as if written into a lesson plan.

You sat up and sighed. "I want you to know how I feel. I don't want you to have questions about my intentions. I want to be fair to you."

I inhaled deeply. I wasn't prepared for where this might be headed. Truly, I was not prepared for any of this.

"I want more than a friendship with you, Mary Beth. I want to take you to dinner. I want to go see a musical with you. I want to get to know you. I know there are obstacles ahead of us, but I think that's okay. I'd ask anyone standing against us to show me a relationship that doesn't have obstacles."

I felt the flames of my feelings rise into my cheeks. I was flattered, certainly, but also a little unsure. What you were saying had been coded into every wish I had made since I was fifteen. Consequently, I knew that I should have been blown away by this development. Instead, I felt something nameless lurking in my mind. Like a stranger, it stood in the dark, awaiting an introduction.

"This is very surreal," I breathed, as I searched for more to say.

"I know. I surely wasn't ready and prepared for this, but it's exciting and I welcome it." I thought I saw honesty there in your eyes, when I looked into the screen of my Mac.

"I wasn't ready either, even though I think I have spent more time thinking about this than you have. But, never as something that stood a real chance at being mutual. It was always just the dreams of a girl who cared about her teacher. A lot," I spoke carefully. The confession worried me, but it felt important to share. I needed you to understand the weight of your words. I wanted you to know where my heart was, so that you might understand its fragility. In retrospect, I think this is the first time I dared to glance at what I stood to lose if this ended poorly.

But you didn't see. Instead, you responded with a familiar phrase, one that was certain to end any questioning for those who consider themselves "believers" like I did. "As long as we continue to seek first the Kingdom, I think He will put everything into place for us."

Later that night, after we had closed our computers, I tucked myself into my lofted bed. I blinked at the ceiling and replayed our conversation. As I did, the shadows in my mind spread, pulling at pieces of my memories. I realized that when you said all of this, you never asked about my feelings. There were no questions about my intentions. You had either known that I would always take your lead, or you forgot to ask. I tend to believe the latter, but again, I remain very generous in my thoughts of you.

I thought you meant it then, that you had not prepared for this moment. The alternative was that you had planned this, and the years of favor and attention were riddled with intent. I think that the truth may lie somewhere in the weeds between the two. You had failed to build the boundaries when they were needed. Therefore, what once was a crush had been allowed to grow. With this new attention from you, its roots deepened until they could not be unearthed with a slight pull. My devotion to you was like an invasive species, growing where it didn't belong, and my girlhood shriveled, unable to sustain itself as it succumbed to this foreign thing.

In these delicate moments when the darkness threatened our peace, I walked the path of ignorance. There was an element of choice in this for me. I know this now, though I will not claim responsibility for trusting you. I wish you had even an ounce of the wisdom that I believed I saw in you. I think if you did, I would be free.

12

Maverick

"If God brings you to it, He will bring you through it."

Eleventh Grade

In all of high school, there is really only one person who was a true friend to me. I had a few other friendships but none that lasted the test of growing up. Maverick was funny, loyal, and tenacious. Maverick deserves the world and if I could, I'd give it to him.

We grew up in a small town in the Midwest. The diversity in our population was essentially nonexistent. I mean to say my town was filled with white, Christian, heterosexual (presenting) individuals. To stray from this was considered reprehensible in our town, which is why Maverick faced such adversity as one of the only individuals brave enough to share his truest self.

Maverick was an outspoken, gay teenager. He was a light that others repeatedly attempted to dim. I loved him and so did you. There were many late nights, after-rehearsal vent sessions, and inside jokes among the three of us. If it matters to you, I do think you did right by Maverick.

One night, Maverick and I sat in the dark school parking lot after a vocal rehearsal. Maverick was never eager to get home. Actually, I think he preferred to be anywhere but home. We would sit in our cars or on the sidewalk until my mom would inevitably call looking for me. This night, we were sitting in his heated car due to the cold. We sang along to one of the *Glee* cast albums, laughing at each other's overly dramatic expressions and voices.

It wasn't until I received the text from my mom, asking for my ETA, that I realized I had forgotten something. "Oh, darn it! Mav, I forgot to grab my choir dress for the competition tomorrow!" I exclaimed.

"Don't freak. Let's see if the door is unlocked. I bet Davis is still in there. He never leaves, I swear." Maverick slid out of his seat and ran to the door to the building. He gave it a jiggle and shrugged in defeat.

"I'll call him," I said as Maverick slid back into the seat. By the fourth ring I turned to Maverick and shook my head. "Shoot, what should we do?"

Maverick laughed and jumped out of the car yelling, "Come on!"

I followed, laughing at Maverick's dramatic run. I followed him behind the building to the courtyard that filled the space between your classroom and us. "Shhhh," Maverick put a finger to his lips and pushed himself against the wall as if he were a spy in a corny movie. It was enough to make me laugh out loud.

I attempted to silence my giggles with a hand over my mouth. I looked at your window, glowing in the dark, abandoned school. You sat at your desk, seemingly planning for the competition the following day. Once again, I was in awe of how beautiful you were and also how alone.

Maverick inched his way closer and knocked loudly on your window before turning and sprinting back to me. To his dismay, you did not even startle. Instead you stood and walked to the window just in time to watch Maverick trip over something in the mud. He landed with a theatrical *splat*.

You spotted me through the window as I doubled over in hysterics at Maverick's misfortune. You were laughing, soundless behind the window, which made me laugh harder. You smiled and tapped at the window. I locked eyes with you and saw you mouth something I couldn't understand as you pointed to the front of the building. I helped Maverick out of the mud and pulled him around to the front of the building, tears streaming down our faces as we gasped for breath between laughs.

When we got to the parking lot, you were standing and shaking your head in mock disapproval. "What are you two doing? Go home!"

"Don't blame me. You didn't answer your phone!" Maverick said, attempting and failing to brush the mud off of his pants. "This one forgot her choir dress."

"Guilty," I said with a shrug. "I'm sorry, I did not tell him to do that, though."

You laughed and used your badge to unlock the door. You held it open and gestured for me to go in, "Well then, go on. You know where it is, right?"

"Yes of course," I sang, as I ran down the hall to your room. I opened the closet in the back of your room, retrieved my dress, and carried it back down the hallway. When I returned, you were leaning casually against the brick of the building. Maverick was retelling the story of his fall, complete with dramatic reenactments as you laughed.

"Got it," I said. "Thanks, Mr. Davis. Sorry about . . . that," gesturing to Maverick, who rolled his eyes.

I grabbed Maverick by the sleeve and tugged him toward his car, which was not where we left it. I scanned the lot, confused. You and I saw it at the same time and shouted in unison, "Maverick, your car!"

Maverick's car rolled backward, slowly picking up speed. I looked over at Maverick, who was frozen with his jaw open like a cartoon character. "Maverick!" I yelled, giving him a little push. He snapped out of it, and in a second was sprinting to his car. He climbed into the driver's side, but not before the car was stopped by the only other obstruction in the parking lot—your car.

I winced as the cars collided with a loud thud. Maverick sat in the car, both hands over his mouth. I looked to you, worried that you were angry with us. Instead, you walked to Maverick, helped him out of his car, and asked, "Are you okay?"

You never asked Maverick to pay for the damage on your car or reprimanded him for leaving his car without putting it in park first. After all, we were just kids, and kids make silly little mistakes, don't they?

Maverick stood by me through every single monumental and mundane moment of high school. When I was inexplicably voted onto Homecoming Court, Maverick took it upon himself to secure my position as Homecoming Queen. He walked the halls for weeks yelling, "Mary Beth Wilson Homecoming Queen 2012," until I was crowned. When I told him I was anxious about being a bad kisser, he kissed me right on the mouth and said, "You've got this, babe." We walked the halls hand in hand. When I was with Maverick, it didn't really matter to me that I had failed to make connections with my peers.

Twelfth Grade

Our sophomore year, Maverick had received a shirt that said *Jesus is not a Homophobe* as a gift. It was a plain, white shirt with black letters and a rainbow fish. There was nothing obscene about this shirt except that it apparently was offensive to suggest Jesus did not hate people who were gay. This was considered such an aggressive message that it had to be remedied immediately. Maverick was called to the principal's office and sent to change.

As you know, the story did not end there. Maverick was unyielding. I am in awe of the next part of his story. Maverick stood his ground and eventually filed a lawsuit against our school for this blatant display of discrimination. By the time the case was scheduled, we were seniors. Every step of that journey he was met with hatred and bullies. Our school was no longer safe for him. He had to use the private bathroom in the office and clung closely to the peers and teachers who supported him. You were one of these pillars for him, and despite my feelings toward you, I am thankful to you for this.

After a long legal battle, Maverick won. It was a huge milestone for our small community, but, as with most progress, it was met with resistance. On the Day of Silence, a day to bring awareness to LGBTQ+ students and the effects of bullying in their schools, Maverick came to school in his shirt. As I drove to school that morning, I saw community members from the local church lining the streets. They had not been allowed on school property but stood in protest on its perimeter, signs in hand. They proclaimed, more or less, that Jesus *was* a homophobe.

Through all of it, you were vocal in your support of Maverick. You encouraged him to be who he was without apology, even when I am sure your administrators wished you would be quiet.

I debated giving you such a heroic story. You did wrong by me, but you were not always wrong. I think this is who you were to most of the people who knew you. A kind, supportive teacher who loved his students and created a safe space for them when their world was unsafe. Many of my peers get to remember you this way. It's why you were so beloved by everyone and why we all trusted you so much. I am jealous of those who do not know what you did. The existence of this man is nothing more than a myth to me now, one I would willingly believe in if I did not know better.

13
Humbled

"I am humbled by the fact that you have even thought of me as more than a friend."

Humble: To lower (someone) in dignity or importance. (*The Oxford English Dictionary*).

I started to write you a story here, but once I found the definition, everything else seemed unimportant. I imagine what it was like for you, when you decided it was okay to pursue me. I wonder when that happened. Was it an event or just the chipping away of your humility that allowed you to walk this path?

Sometimes, I imagine your conversations. Did you confide in anyone before you told me how we would be alone together and maintain our purity? Did you confess your past to the women you dated after me? Did they forgive you? I have many questions, but very few answers.

I wonder if you considered the consequences of a relationship with a former student. You had to know it would not work out between us, so what was your plan? Did you have one? I assume not, because you never asked for my discretion. You never implied that I *should* keep this secret. Maybe you trusted me because you knew

I had done it before. I had kept your secrets faithfully. I'm sorry I cannot stay quiet anymore. I am sorry for the way this story will humble you further.

What I do know is this: You were correct in what you said. You were humbled. If you had dignity or a sense of importance, you would not have risked yourself for a teenage girl with very little to offer you. Though I feel sorry that it had to happen this way, I will not apologize for the consequences of your actions. I've done enough of that.

14

Libido (and Other Words)

"It would be nice to see you in person."

High School

It's such a tender time, the years we spend as teenagers. While we hold the inherent innocence of youth in our minds, our bodies propel us into adolescence. Without our consent, we are thrust into a sea of hormones and given very little help to navigate the uncharted waters. This is especially true for those of us who grew up in the church. These feelings are immediately labeled as sin, and we are told to shove them into the farthest corner of our mind until that day when we slide a ring onto our finger and pledge our bodies to another.

I remember the floods of these new feelings vividly because I had to work so hard to hide them away. I have always been terribly competitive when it came to being "good." Thus, when the kids my age were sneaking away to make out under the bleachers, I was getting dumped over AOL Instant Messenger. In junior high, boys claimed if I really liked them I would have let them kiss me. Meanwhile, girls would taunt me and call me names like "freezer," poking fun at what they saw as a lack of sexuality in my nature. By the time I was in high school, I was preceded by my reputation as a "goodie goodie."

Once, I remember sitting in physics class listening to a couple of boys talking about a girl who had sent a shirtless photo in what she believed to be a private exchange. Unfortunately, they were sharing the picture with each other and laughing over the shape of her breasts. A boy named Joey commented on her nipples and I scoffed. He turned to me, amused.

"That wasn't very nice," I said simply.

Instead of moving on, he responded rather loudly, directing his voice to his group of friends. "It's okay, Mary, you're safe. I can't even picture you naked. You're too innocent. Actually, I can't even imagine you ever having sex."

I turned back to him, and said with all the confidence I could muster, "That wasn't very nice either."

The thing about reputations in a small town is, they stick. With little input of my own, my story was written for me. What nobody seemed to know was that I wanted a boy to try to kiss me. Very few took the chance, but when they did, I wished they would push against my reservations. I hoped someone might test my limits, just a little bit. I had the same desires as all of the kids my age, I just kept them buried away. The truth is, I was terrified of the things I felt, and the more everyone seemed to "know" me, the more I convinced myself they were right.

I don't think any adult, including myself now at twenty-nine, knows how to handle these delicate conversations perfectly. However, I can tell you one thing I do know for certain: The responsibility of educating teens on this topic cannot and should not fall simply to *anyone*.

Eleventh Grade

Once, in music history, you were teaching us to analyze a song. For whatever reason, this song was "Bust a Move" by Young MC. We were given a single verse, printed out on paper, and tasked with counting syllables and finding patterns. This assignment was partner work and, to my despair, Maverick was absent. Instead, I found myself paired with a boy in my grade named Michael. Michael was a tall, ginger-haired football player with icy blue eyes and a jawline that could cut glass. He was very cute and he knew it. We sat together on the top riser. I attempted to complete the assignment while Michael attempted to keep me giggling at his ridiculousness. We must have been disruptive because you approached us, arms crossed in disapproval.

"Oh, are you finished already?" you asked, climbing the risers and sitting on the other side of me.

"Nah," Michael laughed, "She was just asking me what *libido* means. I told her I'd tell her, but I don't want to ruin her innocence."

I rolled my eyes at Michael and turned back to you. You looked . . . amused. "Oh God, what is it?" I asked.

"It's not going to *ruin* your innocence." You rolled your eyes and pointed to the paper on my lap. "Libido just means sex drive."

"Oh . . . " I said, trying to process what that meant.

You must have noticed my confusion because you continued, "You know, like, your biological desire for sex." You turned to Michael, who was laughing because, after all, he was a seventeen-year-old boy and his teacher just said the word *sex*. "Don't laugh, it's science." You shook your head and continued, "Did you know it differs between men and women? Men have an especially high libido from, well this," you gestured to Michael, who shrugged in agreement, "until they are in their thirties. Conveniently, that's when women see an increase in libido." You laughed, as if that was funny. Per usual, I didn't get the joke.

Another day, in choir, Maverick and I sat on the bottom riser waiting for class to start. While some students trickled in the door, others chatted on the risers. You sat in front of us, reviewing the music at the piano. From behind us, I could hear a group of tenors being stupid and loud. Over the course of minutes, this turned into full-blown roughhousing. You got up from your seat and started to approach them, ready to intercede.

I turned to them, hoping to save you the trouble. "Stop jacking off, you guys."

Maverick immediately started cackling, and you covered your mouth to hide your chuckle.

Maverick gasped, through fits of laughter. "Oh my GOD! You can't say that MB!"

"What? I'm telling them to stop messing around!" I started to panic when I saw you shaking your head.

"That's not what that means," you said gently.

"Wait, it isn't? What does it mean?" I asked.

You and Maverick exchanged a glance before evidently deciding to tread carefully.

"I am not going to tell her," you said, arms up. "Maverick, you can whisper it to her."

Maverick leaned over and whispered, "It means masturbating, Mary Beth."

I stared at him, then shook my head and whispered back, "I don't know what that means."

He cackled again and you stepped in closer and lowered your voice so the others wouldn't hear. "You know . . . it's something your male peers do. A lot."

Maverick leaned in closer and made a crude motion with his hands, miming the meaning.

I was embarrassed to admit that I still did not understand. I was seventeen years old and I had no idea what any of it meant until Maverick leaned in and explained it to me, in detail.

I wrinkled my nose in disgust as I realized what I had said. "Oh my gosh. I am so sorry." I looked up at you, panicked. My face felt like it was surely melting from the embarrassment.

You just smiled and shook your head. "Don't be, kid. You didn't know any better."

In the late winter of my senior year, we took a weekend trip north for Thespian State Conference. You had agreed to be the chaperone and I was thrilled. I spent hours in your passenger seat as we drove. We weren't alone—Maverick, our friend Katie, and Maverick's boyfriend, Jake, sat cramped together in the back. As you drove, what had started as easy listening turned into all of us taking turns belting out show tunes. After a stretch of this, you mandated a break. I don't blame you; we were pretty obnoxious. A few quiet moments passed before Jake yelled out, pointing to a sign on the road. "Adventure Awaits! In my pants." You rolled your eyes and I giggled, as the back seat crew launched themselves into a fit of hysterics.

This game continued through the next hour of the trip. Eventually, you started playing. I remember thinking it was inappropriate, but

I wasn't uncomfortable with it. After all, that's what made you my favorite teacher; you weren't worried about the should and should nots of teaching. Around lunch time, we stopped at a mall. The game continued in hushed tones, as we walked through the hall in search of the food court. We passed several opportune stores for this game, but I never made the joke myself. I just listened. "Victoria's Secret . . . in my pants," Maverick hissed, eliciting a burst of laughter.

You leaned in closer to me and whispered, "I can't say that one out loud. I have my limits." You were pointing at the adjoining store, Pink.

I giggled as you put a finger to your lips, hushing me. You tilted your head toward our peers, implying this one was not for the group. This joke was just for me.

Whether you want to accept this or not, the truth is that our relationship was built when my world was filled with hormones and budding sexuality. During that time as your student, I caught myself daydreaming about you. Sometimes while you stood at the front of the class my imagination would slip away from my control. I'd find myself envisioning what it would be like to share a kiss with you, or more. I wondered what it would be like to be with you. These little trips always ended with an abrupt snap to reality and overwhelming waves of guilt. I was left ashamed. Nevertheless, that little spark of curiosity never died.

College—Year Two

A few short years later, in college, I sat on a piano bench with my legs curled into my chest. It was well past midnight, so I had escaped to the little chapel on campus while my peers slept. The only light in the building came from the street lights outside. I watched as the glow danced over the pews, shadowed by the swaying leaves. We had been on the phone for over two hours, and you had finally asked if I could imagine our relationship becoming something more than what it was.

"I can. I mean, I already have," I confessed.

"Me too," you said, softly. "I care about you. Of course, I did when you were a student, but that was how I care for all of my students. Now . . . " You let the words fall away for a moment before regaining the confidence to continue. "This time, I would, I mean I could, imagine myself kissing you." You took a breath, "Could you? I mean, would you kiss me back?"

If it weren't for the audible thud of my heart, I might have believed myself to be a ghost watching her own dream from above. "I would," I breathed.

During this part of our story, you were always far away, living your life in Portland. Consequently, this question was purely hypothetical, and for that I am grateful. I am so thankful you couldn't reach me when you decided that you wanted me. I think if you had, you could have held me there forever. You once said you wished you could have been closer, but I am so grateful that you were far away.

15
Teacher's Pet

"... even still my heart beams with gladness at the thought."

Twelfth Grade

I once thought I was your favorite student. If I am honest, a part of me wants to believe I may have been. Worse, I delusionally find myself hoping I still might be. I am a competitive perfectionist, which is why I cannot deny that I was predisposed to seek your favor. If grades were given for being a perfect victim, I'd have received an A-plus.

Because I was once a teacher, I am fully aware that staying home from work sometimes is more work than showing up anyway. Whatever the case, a teacher has to weigh the choice carefully. If I was too sick to attend school, surely I was too sick to write out several pages of detailed sub plans at 5 a.m., text my friends to gather/copy my materials, and then sit in anxiety that they would not find coverage for my class. Being away from school was always such a burden. Because of my experience, I do empathize with the decisions you made. However, I feel obligated to call them into question. Perhaps if you had not done what you did later, I would not be so critical. Unfortunately, I have been forced to scrutinize your behaviors and decisions. Selfishly, I want to bring you with me on this journey.

One September day my senior year, your music history lesson wrapped a bit early. While the rest of the class left quickly, eager to be the first out of the traffic jam that was dismissal, I stayed behind. I was always looking for little moments to chat with you. You shuffled papers from behind your desk while I thought of a reason to stay. After a minute, I decided to ask about your plans for your newest project, the show choir, which you had only announced earlier in the week. You slid some papers aside and took a casual seat on your desk, gesturing for me to sit in your chair. I slid my backpack off my shoulder and sat. I noticed the way you smiled, as if my interest brought you joy. You told me the outline, admitting that we had no budget for a choreographer so you would be tasked with planning and instructing our movement. The absurdity of this made me laugh, which made your smile grow. I watched as it reached your eyes with a soft crinkle.

"What about you?" you asked, pressing your foot against my leg playfully.

"What do you mean?" I laughed and pushed your foot away.

"I told you my plans for the future. What are yours?" Maybe I imagined the sincerity in your voice, but something about the way you were looking down at me made me believe you really cared to know.

"Oh, well, I am set on my college and definitely want to major in education, but I just don't know what I want to teach." I groaned and slid down in my seat. I had been feeling very defeated. Choosing a path for my future felt like such an unfair, impossible task at sixteen.

"That's not true." You held my gaze, eyes narrowed in suspicion. You always seemed to have the power to see right through me, and that skill made me feel especially vulnerable.

"Well, what if it's not the right fit? What if I'm no good at it? What if I can never master the theory? You know how much I hate music theory!" I buried my face in my hands, embarrassed and exasperated. The deadline to apply for the music program was quickly approaching, yet I seemed to be spiraling further from the decision.

There was a pause as you took in my outburst. Then, you slapped your hands on your knees. "Hey! What if you taught my class? I can teach you a few things after school this week. Maybe the next time I am absent, you can be my sub! Oh! Jake will play piano for you, so you won't even have to worry about that. What do you say?"

I looked up at you and felt heat rush to my face. You had lowered yourself so that our faces were very close. Inspiration brought a sparkle into your eyes and lit my soul. I thought you were stunning.

I agreed, and over the next week we met a few times to talk about segmenting the piece and running parts. You taught me the minimum of "conducting" and we reviewed the time signatures for our music. Like you promised, the next time you were absent, I received a message from you.

```
Going to be out tomorrow - ready? :) - D
```

I was immediately excited and nervous, but also acutely aware that you wouldn't be there to watch me shine. I hoped to make you proud anyway.

```
Not really, but I will do my best for you. What's
the plan?
```

The next day, I showed up to class with a page of notes you had sent me the previous night. I had printed them at the library during my study period. The sub sat behind the computer with a book open in her hands. When the bell rang, she didn't bother getting up from her seat. "Alright, who is Mary Beth?" she read from the paper on your desk.

I pretended to be oblivious to the way my classmates groaned as I put my hand in the air. "I'm here," I said.

"Well, my sub plan says you are in charge. Go for it, kiddo." She gestured to the piano and spent the rest of the class reading her book and munching through a bag of pretzels.

I taught your class that day and almost every day that you were away from school my senior year. I'm not sure that it had the effect that you had hoped. Instead, my peers grew to resent me for yet again stealing your favor, and the discomfort of teaching them may have led to my choice to pursue early childhood education instead of music.

There was no escaping the fact that I may have stood out to you among the other students. In October, we were tagged in a photograph that had been posted to the official social media page for our town's annual fall festival. We had attended together because the a cappella group was performing. I was honored to sing the lead vocals for what was quite possibly the largest crowd of my career in music. Unfortunately, what was once a shining moment has twisted into darkness, alongside all of my memories with you.

After the performance we sat in the crowd to watch the other groups. I do not remember this moment, but the photograph of us lives in my mind. You and I are sitting next to each other in the third row. For whatever reason, the rest of the group is seated in the second. You are dressed in a light blue button-down shirt that is tucked into cuffed blue jeans. If I look closely, I can glimpse the tiny sailboats on your navy socks. I am in my favorite yellow sweater, my dark curls falling wildly behind me. The students in the front row are looking at you, but you are not looking back. You are looking at me, smiling with an open mouth, seemingly mid-laugh. Your head is tilted toward mine, as if you told a joke just for me. My head is thrown back in what I imagine was my own belly laugh. I saved the picture to my phone because I loved the way you were looking at me. I couldn't explain it at the time, but it made me feel incredibly special. Now when I see the photo my heart aches for that girl.

There were times it was less subtle. For example, when we attended the annual choral competition my senior year, you told the entire alto section that we were counting solely on my sight-reading skills. In fact, you told them that it was better not to sing at all than to sing incorrect notes over me.

Then, there was that time Maverick asked if you had ever been truly mad at your students. When you answered, "Of course," he feigned shock.

"Okay, have you been mad at me specifically?" he asked, clearly hoping to make you squirm.

"You? Absolutely," you responded, without pausing to think.

Maverick laughed. "That's fair honestly, but surely you've never been mad at MB, have you?"

This time you did pause. You looked at me and I was filled with a rush of emotion. I hoped you would not lie, but I also worried I may die of disappointment if you said yes.

When you finally spoke, you did so carefully. "No, not mad exactly. I have been frustrated with her though."

I fought the urge to press while Maverick blazed ahead. "What kind of answer is that? Frustrated? When?"

I looked at you, silently urging you to expand. You shrugged, "Oh, every now and again. Like when she won't try something new because she's worried she'll be bad at it. Or when she won't stand up for herself. Her inability to make a choice that requires any level of risk drives me crazy sometimes. But I find it especially frustrating when she doesn't recognize how special and talented she is."

Your response felt so strangely intimate that I remember it all these years later. Everyone else moved on from this moment, assessing the times you had been angry with various students. As it turned out, it would seem as though you had been angry with everyone but me. I don't remember the rest of that conversation because I was too busy processing the feeling of closeness your response had evoked. It was clear that you knew me deeply and gave words to the things about myself that even I had not been able to name.

Your favor could be noted implicitly, but there was one time that it was explicit. After graduation, I stopped at the choir room to return the folder and music I had used for the ceremony. You were there, packing away your equipment for the summer. I had been crying and my cheeks were streaked with my makeup. I knew I looked like a wreck, but I hadn't bothered fixing myself because I had yet to stop crying. I walked to you, teary-eyed, and handed you my folder.

You laughed at the intensity of my feelings. "Hey kid, it's not such a bad thing. This is not the ending you think it is."

That just made me cry harder. "It is though, isn't it? I could leave this place and these people behind in a second, you know that. But I will never get a chance to do music like this ever again." I choked over the last word as a sob bubbled in my throat.

"Oh kid." You stepped closer and pulled me to you. You held me for a moment as I reminded myself to take deep breaths. Your hand traced gentle circles on my back and I let myself relax into your comfort. "You will never stop finding ways to make music a part of your life. You can't. It's a part of you." Your hands moved to my shoulders, and you pulled away so that you could look me in the eyes. Like a CD that has been overplayed, the next thing you said has stayed on repeat in my memories.

"You are the most talented young woman in your class. No, I take that back. You are the most talented kid that I have ever directed in my ten years as a teacher. The only real tragedy here would be if you chose to leave that behind. Promise me you won't leave it behind."

I sighed and gave a sad smile as you turned and walked to your desk. I ran one hand across the wetness on my cheeks as you returned to place a tissue in the other. "Thank you," I said, "for this." I held up the tissue before using it to blot at my running mascara. "But also for . . . everything. It may be weird to say this, but I wouldn't know who I am if it weren't for you. I am scared that I will lose that when I leave. I never had friends here, but I always had you."

You looked down at me, eyes glassy with emotion. "I'll miss you, but you'll be just fine out there, kid."

I went away to college and tasked myself with paving the way to my future. I tried to stay in the campus choir but eventually was forced to give it up for my academic schedule. Eventually, I became a kindergarten teacher. My therapist once asked if I could see myself speaking to my students the way you spoke to me. I laughed at her and reminded her that my students were five and six, not teenagers. She smiled patiently and said, "Yes, that is true. But, the point remains that they are still children and you are their teacher. You were a child and he was your teacher. Would you ever tell one of your students that they were your favorite? Would you tell the others to sit back and watch the smartest kid?"

At the time, I didn't give her much credit. I thought she was making wild comparisons. Then, I became a director for a high school theater program. I formed relationships with students over many evenings spent directing, but it never once occurred to me to tell them my secrets. There were clear standouts in the cast, but I was so careful to disperse my attention evenly. Because of you, I panicked every time I felt myself getting close to a student.

It's true, high schoolers are different from five-year-olds. They have a wit and charm that makes them appear much older. But then any moment, they might do something so foolish that in a flash you are reminded of their youth. I understand now how delicate the line is, but because of you, I stand five steps back. Before I took the position, I sat down with the music director for our show. I expressed my concerns and my fears that I might unknowingly do what you did to me. It felt inevitable, like I might not be capable of rebuilding the boundaries you had destroyed. She listened to my story and my fears. Then, she nodded thoughtfully and said, "That right there is how I know you will be okay. Because you are thoughtful, intentional, and committed to being better."

16
Women
"You have shown me how to treat a woman."

W hen I was a girl, I dreamed of womanhood. I would often sit at my parents' table with a bowl of cereal, watching an episode of *Full House*, while fantasizing about silky nightgowns, black coffee, and crossword puzzles. I've never felt my age. I often wonder if any woman has.

If you ask the question, "when does a girl become a woman," you will get a variety of answers. While society might suggest womanhood begins with various identifying ages or significant events, most of us will admit that we do not have an answer. Womanhood, it turns out, is not so simple to define.

I am hopeful that now, in the year 2024, we are able to agree that womanhood is not a switch that flips on the moment a girl starts to bleed. Although legislation seems to disagree, that is a conversation for another time. I got my first period in sixth grade. I was your student at the time, though I am not sure you noticed me. It was a terrifying time, but thanks to a girl in my class who agreed to accompany me to ask for help, all was well. My English teacher sent me to the bathroom with a pad from her personal stash and excused me to call my mom. Thank goodness for women, honestly. The world is not set up to receive us as we are, so we have to work together. In the months that followed, I navigated this new cycle rather poorly. I put in tampons so wrong it hurt, bled through several of my favorite clothes, and felt completely helpless when it came to the pain and hormonal shifts of it all. Worse, the boys at the time were brutal. It became a daily occurrence that they would take turns raiding my belongings and stealing my "sanitary items." They'd stick them to each other's lockers and slip them into backpacks. It was as if my human needs were a dirty joke. When I complained about this behavior, I was told that boys matured much slower than girls. And so, I learned to be more discreet. From this young age, I was taught to be small, to rely on myself, and to shield the boys from my reality. I do not believe I became a woman at the age of twelve. Instead, I took on my new responsibilities without protest. Maybe womanhood is the result of repeated, small nudges.

Or perhaps womanhood begins at the age of consent. Allegedly, on their sixteenth birthday, children are considered to be capable of making choices for their bodies. Although that does not entirely apply to girls, or women, or anyone with the anatomy capable of carrying life at any age. There is disparity in agreement on these laws between states. Additionally, the laws are written with disclaimers about consenting to individuals past the age of eighteen, or sometimes nineteen. You will not find me arguing against these laws; they exist for several reasons, one being that we live in a world of predators. However, I will say that this stage of our journey is nuanced. As children, we sit awkwardly in health class where we are taught about abstinence, STDs, and childbirth. Yet, I cannot recall a lesson about pleasure, bodily autonomy, and the spectrum of sexuality. I remember this time in my life, comparing notes with the boys after we split to talk about our bodies. It seemed the boys were taught to "wrap it up," while we had been taught to "just say no." Boys were taught about managing their drive for sex, yet we were taught about the repercussions of childbirth on our young bodies. Repeatedly, the responsibility of adulthood is thrust on women, while men are allowed grace when their boyhood lingers.

Not long after this, we reach another landmark in our journey toward adulthood. On my eighteenth birthday, I woke up to the smell of cinnamon and the sight of my college roommate, Nikki, holding a to-go box of my favorite pancakes. I can't say I felt any different that day. Regardless of my feelings, the law said that I was an adult. I could open credit cards, put my car in my own name, and make my own medical decisions. I did none of those things. Truthfully, I never experienced the liberation that I had expected to accompany this birthday. Instead, I found myself walking into a new cage. Unlike the restraints of childhood, this enclosure provided gaps of sunlight and the illusion of freedom. It is possible that I would have transformed in my eighteenth year of life had the church not put its thumb on my womanhood.

When I was nineteen, I thought I had the answers to womanhood. I know now that I had been on the threshold of adulthood, with one foot in adolescence. I worked hard to mold myself into the woman I had been instructed to be by my church. I was obedient, humble, and pure. I had thrown out my crop tops and purchased a one-piece swimsuit to protect my brothers in Christ, which apparently was my responsibility. Meanwhile, I began to notice the way I looked over my shoulder when I walked alone. I detected the change in my pace if I heard a man behind me, no matter how benign he might actually be. I saw the way men were never questioned for their dress, or even their behaviors. The disparity was so prevalent it was impossible to ignore. This is the year I began to question my own beliefs about women.

Now, I see womanhood as a spectrum. There is no answer. There was no chrysalis, no moment in which I emerged transformed. Instead, my journey to womanhood was a long one, filled with revelations and regressions. Consequently, I no longer require an answer to this question. I would suggest that if you need to question whether she is a woman or a girl, you already have an answer.

By thirty-four, you had had so many opportunities to learn how to treat a woman. I think of them often, these women in your life, both past and present. I would say that I am shocked to find you felt yourself less than competent when it came to women, but I am not. I think that may be why you chose to cast your attention on a girl.

I find it endlessly fascinating the way you so confidently called me a woman at nineteen. It makes me wonder when you experienced the shift, which, in turn, forces me to consider that you did not. If you had a hand in my girlhood, you cannot experience me as a woman. At least not in the way you sought to experience me.

Instead of teaching you about women, I think I validated your thoughts that finding a woman is like finding a harmony. Many options exist, all are lovely, but none can stand alone. I wish you had understood that nothing good or right can come from looking to a girl to teach you about women. But I see now that despite what you said, you had no intentions of learning. Not then, anyway.

Unfortunately, I fear this may be lost on you. I am aware that you lack the capacity to learn from me, even now that I am grown. You considered yourself an expert in the field of education, but you only played student to your almighty God and fellow man. I think if you ever learned how to treat a woman in your thirty-four years, you would have immediately denied yourself the pleasure of my attention. If I had truly taught you about women at nineteen, you would have apologized and left me alone.

I often find myself wondering what you might think of the woman that I have become. In response to this, my therapist informed me that our brain freezes at the time of a trauma. It was such a profound realization. This might explain why when I think of you, I feel like a child again. I wonder why, after all these years, you added me on Facebook. *Was it to watch me from afar?* I cannot comprehend how you have not provided me with the apology I feel I am owed. *Are you mad at me?* I wish to know if you feel shame about what you did. *Did I deserve to be hidden?* I often feel like a jaded teen, experiencing heartbreak and lacking the emotional maturity to move forward. After all, you did not guide me into womanhood; instead you took a piece of my girlhood. I am not sure if you stole this or if I gave it to you willingly, but I wish I could take it back.

17

Peace

"I am so happy that Christ is first between you and I. That gives me such comfort and peace."

College—Year Two

The student union on my campus was a large, multistory building. The first floor was filled with tiny outlets for campus essentials. Just past the campus bookstore, there were several small food service areas. Large tables stretched across the open space, much like a cafeteria. This floor was for socializing, filled with the buzzing of young adults either waiting in the incredibly long line at Starbucks on their way to class, or chatting with friends over smoothies and fried chicken. I always spent as little time as possible on the first floor.

The second floor was much more conducive to studying. There were several small tables along a balcony that overlooked the wooded lawn and paved brick pathway of the campus. If you walked back you would find couches and chairs set as if in several small living rooms. There was a 70 percent chance you would find a student stretched out and fully asleep here. The second floor also happened to be the home to my "pop-up" church.

One Sunday in February I made my way through a brutal, chilly wind. Though most of my legs were protected by my knee-length parka, I silently cursed my decision to wear a dress. Admittedly, my thin, sheer tights were a sad attempt at blocking the cold. It was early and the sun had yet to rise. The only light came from the glow of the streetlights along the brick path. I rushed along until I made it through the doors of the union. I was filled with immediate relief from the wind, shielded within the breezeway. I attempted to put myself back together, tugging at my curls as I shuffled up the stairs to the student ballroom.

The ballroom was transformed weekly into an approximation of a megachurch. The floor was filled with chairs. Hundreds to be exact, lined in several neat rows facing a large stage that was both assembled and packed away into a truck by 8 p.m. A large screen stretched along the back of the stage, showing slides to promote upcoming retreats, life group events, and prayer requests. A table set with donuts and coffee sat along the back wall, manned by eager evangelists, prowling the attendees for a new face to pull into the folds of our community.

Unfortunately, I was one of these eager evangelists hoping to become a staff member one day. I was interning for the church as the head of the "First Impressions" team. This meant I showed up before the pastors or the worship teams. I pulled boxes from a truck and set up tables for selling the newest approved study books and Bibles. I coordinated the team members and delegated tasks such as getting donuts from the campus Dunkin' Donuts, setting chairs in long, neat rows, hanging signs/banners, and brewing an obscene amount of coffee. Before the service began, I gathered my team to pray over the space and the students who would stumble through our doors, entreating that they may find a home in our community. Then, I would stand in the doorway, a smile plastered to my sleepy face, and greet every single one of the hundreds of students attending each of our three Sunday services.

On this particular day, I set up my tables and directed my team. We said our prayer, and I snuck to the back to grab a cup of hot coffee before the students started to arrive for service. I had saved a seat in the back and made my way over as the worship music began. From the moment the lights dimmed and the stage illuminated, I was in my zone. I closed my eyes and sang out to a God I once believed in. When our pastor took the stage, I bowed my head obediently. I sat as we said our amens. I opened my purple journal and started to doodle the sermon title at the top of the page in big, bold letters: "PEACE."

I sat for an hour and listened to a conventionally attractive, former college athlete turned head pastor speak on finding our peace in the Lord. I wrote the highlights in neat, organized bullet points, as I did every week.

- Seek the Kingdom of God above all else, and live righteously, and he will give you everything you need. (Matthew 6:33)
  - In all things, pray → no decision can be made without prayer
  - Get in His Word
  - If you are not at peace, ask yourself, are you seeking earthly or heavenly desires?
- Sin is a thief who comes to steal your peace
  - We can only be at peace when we are saying **no** to sin
  - Identify weakness and put protections in place → ask, "What comes one, or two, steps before the sin?" AVOID TRIGGERS!!
- Surround yourself with others who follow Jesus
  - Pray together!! For where two or three are gathered together in my name, I am there among them (Matthew 18:20)
  - Surround yourself with those who put Christ first
    - That goes for relationships too! See 2 Corinthians 6:14–18 <3
  - Hold each other accountable → there is PEACE in freedom from sin!!!

As the pastor invited us to bow our heads in closing prayer, I tucked my journal into my bag and tiptoed back to the doors in order to offer a friendly goodbye to everyone on the way out. Once the area had generally cleared, I cleaned up the tables, rearranged the donuts, and brewed a fresh batch of coffee. As I waited for the light to indicate the coffee was done, I checked my phone. My heart did a little jump when I saw that I had a message from you.

Good morning! Not gonna lie—TIRED. How was church?

I smiled to myself as I typed a response. I am not sure if you ever understood how much it meant to me to know that you thought of me enough to message first. But you should know, you never thought of me first. You couldn't possibly, because I was always thinking about you.

SO good! Today was all about peace. The Lord definitely knew what I needed!

I finished my tasks and prepared to start the process of organizing my team for the next service. As I waited for the others to join in our circle for our pre-service prayer, a response came through from you.

Would love to hear about it. Talk later? :)

I typed a quick response to let you know I would be stuck hanging out in the union during the evening service but would text you later. Then I busied myself with my preparations for the second service. I spent the next chunk of my day journaling, napping, and reading through my educational psychology textbook over a quick lunch.

I returned to the union for evening service. I made quick work of tidying the tables and grabbed a new box of handouts from the truck. Finally, as the light dimmed and music began to blare in the ballroom, I settled into a quiet nook at the back of the union to wait out the service. I sent you a text to let you know I was ready to talk and waited anxiously for your reply.

Check ur email! Just sent you something . . . will call in a few!

I smiled and opened my laptop to find your email. The subject read simply, "Devo." What followed was an attachment to a devotional focused on giving control to God. You had added a few of your thoughts and a hope to expand upon this over the phone "later." Just as I finished reading, my phone started to buzz.

"Hi!" I answered, perhaps a little too enthusiastically.

"Well, hello there! It's good to hear your voice. How are you this evening?"

I felt bubbles rise in my chest at your words. It always felt incredibly special to be someone who brought "good" feelings into your life. It was like all I had ever wanted to be to you was finally, fully accessible. "I'm great, just a bit tired. It's been a long day for me with church. What about you?" I asked.

"Better now," you said through a light laugh. "I won't bore you with my life. I'll just say this: Talking with you is the highlight."

If I had bubbles before, there was now an outright chemical reaction occurring in my veins at being called the highlight of your day. I put my hand over my chest, hoping to ease the buzz so that you wouldn't hear it in my voice. "You never bore me," I insisted.

You paused, but I imagined the slow smile spreading over your face. I wondered if you were curled up on a couch like I was. Were you dressed in your typical fashion or had you opted for a more casual choice like sweatpants? Did you even own sweatpants? I laughed internally at the mental image this evoked.

"Did you read the devotional for today?" you asked.

"I actually just finished it. It went really well with the sermon from today. I sent you the link, by the way, in case you want to watch."

"I saw, thank you!" you exclaimed. "I think the Lord is trying to speak to us, don't you?"

Your use of the word "us" felt surreal. How could it be that there was an "us" at all? This all felt like a dream. I was not ready to put words to my own thoughts, so I passed that responsibility back to you. After all, I was hopeful that you were a man who could lead me in the Spirit. "I do. I would love to hear how He is speaking to you."

"Great question, Mary Beth. He is saying a lot to me right now, but it can all be summarized rather simply: God is in control. My life has felt a bit out of my control lately, and I have wondered if this new friendship, or relationship, with you was the right path. In my prayers lately I find myself asking God, 'Why? Why this? Why now?'"

I sucked in a breath. You were either being led to or away from me, and I would have accepted either one. I would have understood if you were having second thoughts about developing a relationship with a former student who was born the year you entered high school. I said a silent prayer that this was not the case, and though I was not sure that I wanted the answer, I asked, "And do you feel like He has answered?"

"He always does," you said, simply. "You know, my will didn't line up with His through most of my life. Yet, he has used my teaching career, my divorce, and other willful decisions I have made to teach me something or help someone else who might be struggling. Even though I make choices with my own will that might counter what God wants for my life, He still finds a way to use them for good. That gives me a lot of confidence in this path we are walking. If we are both prayerful and submissive to God and we trust in His sovereignty, He will use us for good. Amen for that!"

Your perspective filled me with hope. This felt like confirmation that you were pursuing me, just as I had desired for so long. I was filled with excitement and something like fear. Though you never said it in so many words, I think you meant that you wanted to see this through. You spoke as though you cared about protecting my heart and would do what it took to ensure you never led me astray. I loved you for that, but I loved the Lord more, so I was compelled to ask, "And how do you tell? The difference I mean. How do you tell whether this is God leading or our own desires?"

You paused, considering my words. You spoke carefully, as if the words were being cast onto glass that may break if not thrown gently. "You don't. I think you just do the best you can and let God do the rest. I have confidence that if we let Him lead in our lives and give control to Him everything will work out according to His mysterious plan." There was another pause and then your tone shifted into something more tender. "I have a lot of peace about you, Mary Beth. You listen to me in a way I have never experienced in my life. No matter where this goes, I will be forever grateful for this time with you."

These words stuck with me long after our conversation ended. That night, I returned to my journal entry about peace. Instead of thoughtful prayers written in frilly letters, I found myself scribbling questions at the bottom of the page.

How do I have peace about this? What will we tell everyone so that they trust us? Will we ever know peace together? Is peace something I have to accept from God, like permission, rather than a feeling I should seek?

I never found the answers to these questions, though you tried. You told me you had a lot of peace about me. It is riddled in the emails and letters that I received from you. It stands as evidence that you were never held accountable for this chapter of our story. How could you be, when you were simply following God? The culpability did not fall on you, but on the Lord. And if that was the case, one might argue that no wrong was done at all. It is so convenient that you can cast the blame for your misjudgment on an entity that cannot speak for itself. What was once a healthy hesitation became an identifiable lack of faith in the Lord's sovereignty. After all, He works everything "for good and not evil." I wonder how many men have followed similar paths in the name of "God's will." I wonder how many women believed them.

If this was God's plan for me, He delights in my torment. If His sovereignty brought you into my life, He is a glutton for my pain. If you did nothing wrong, I am at fault for my own suffering.

But hey, I am glad you had peace about me. I have never known peace about you.

18

To Death

"I think of you daily."

I am back in choir, once again in my womanhood. You are directing the choir in a song I cannot recall. I am angry that you are here. I was supposed to be back to sing with the alumni and you are not supposed to be here. You ask to see me after rehearsal, and I am filled with both rage and sadness at the thought of speaking to you again. When I approach, I notice the lines on your face. You look tired and my heart softens, just a little. You recommend a private lesson with you, and I respond that it would be inappropriate. I say that I am uncomfortable around you and wish to never be asked to be alone with you again. I do not trust you anymore. You break. What starts as a soft cry turns to a sob, through which you utter apologies. My heart goes limp and suddenly I am holding you. I am stroking your dark hair as you rest against my chest. I forgive you, of course I do. You are grateful but when you pull away I am compelled to speak. I ask you—rather, I plead with you—to tell me what you want from me. You tell me to look around. The walls are covered in handwritten letters that spell "love," scribbled in several sizes and fonts. I cry as I notice an urn, sitting against the far wall.

I awaken before I can ask you what it means. Instead, I write it down and share it with my therapist. She suggests that I mourn you like a death. I don't disagree.

19
Secrets

"When I was able to share . . ."

Twelfth Grade

My senior year, I called you my best friend. I know it is unhealthy. I mean that's why I have a story to tell, isn't it? You and I had built a relationship that bred trust over our years together. You used to joke that vocal lessons often became therapy lessons. I found this to be true, with both you and my private vocal teacher, Mr. Black. Yet, there was a considerable difference between the two relationships. Only in one of these did the roles ever reverse, and I found myself playing the therapist.

By the fall of my senior year, you and I had seen each other at our best, and we had worked together through exhaustion. You had seen me through breakups, friendship rifts, and performance anxieties. You offered compassion, wisdom, and occasionally the tough love I had needed. This was the nature of our relationship and I would say that even this level of connection was relatively harmless. Until it wasn't.

On a Friday in late September, we sat in your room together. We had spent the past few hours rehearsing with our a cappella group. I had become aware of a change in you over the past few weeks that had become of increasing concern to me. Your laugh was shallow and your eyes were sunken. The lighthearted nature I had come to expect from you was scarcely present, and in its place I noticed a lingering sadness.

For whatever reason, I felt comfortable staying behind after my peers had left at the conclusion of our rehearsal. I moved slowly, pretending to fuss with my music until the last of my peers had disappeared out the door. When I looked up, you were sitting behind the piano, head in your hands.

I'm not entirely sure where I discovered the audacity to approach you that day. Perhaps it was because you appeared so vulnerable, like a wounded animal. I stood and walked toward you, taking a seat in the chair that sat next to the bench. You didn't move much, but sighed and rolled your head so that our eyes met. The sadness was palpable.

"Hey, Mr. Davis, you haven't been yourself lately." I paused, slightly shocked with my own boldness. I continued, "Everyone is starting to notice and we are worried about you. Is everything alright?" I asked softly.

"Don't worry about me, kid. I'll be okay." You sighed and turned your gaze to the window. You didn't ask me to leave, so I didn't. I stayed with you, silent company until I started to feel that maybe I should leave you alone.

I stood but didn't take a step away from you just yet. "You will be. Whatever is going on, you will be alright, right?" I said. In hindsight, I lacked the perspective to understand that there are no circumstances in which a student can fill this space for a teacher. At least, not when they should.

"You are very intuitive, Mary Beth Wilson," you said, turning back to me. "I've been going through something in my personal life. I try not to let it affect my teaching. I'm sorry if it has."

I melted back into my seat, taking your confession as an invitation to stay. I slid my backpack to the floor and leaned forward, hoping you might notice my eagerness to listen. "I think that's an unrealistic expectation. You're human, after all."

A sad smile flickered across your face, but it was gone in a moment. You shook your head. "I can't. I can't show it though. I'm in such an impossible situation, Mary Beth." You paused, looking away as you gathered your thoughts before turning back to me deci-sively. "If I tell you something, can it stay between us?"

I nodded, perhaps too enthusiastically, trying to sell you on my sincerity. "Of course, I won't say a word."

"I think my marriage is over."

The confession fell from you like a weight through sweaty palms. I felt it suck the air from my lungs with a sigh. It made sense now, all of the little changes I had noticed in you over the past few weeks. The way you sat crumpled behind the piano, instead of commanding the attention of the room as you had previously. The lines of worry were etched into your face. I felt that I understood your exhaustion. It wasn't that you suddenly lacked the stamina for a loaded schedule of teaching extracurriculars. You were weary.

I searched your eyes, trying to grasp what it was you wanted from me. In that moment, I wished I knew who you needed so that I could become her. "Oh, Mr. Davis," I said simply.

"It's okay. This is life." You shrugged. "Sometimes it just doesn't work, despite how much you try. If she doesn't want to be with me, I can't make her."

I looked out the window. Perhaps I hoped to find the answer to your adult problems. They certainly did not exist in my teenage mind. Instead of finding a suitable reply or sage advice, I became lost in my own thoughts. *How could I make this okay? Why had you picked me to carry this secret? Would you stop me if I hugged you now?* Somewhere in the building a door slammed, breaking the deafening silence and pulling me back into my place, here with you. I looked over to find your gaze remained transfixed outside, as if watching something in the empty courtyard.

Finally, you sighed. "I can't tell anyone here. She has taken this space from me. I asked her to resign. It seems fair, right? She gave up on me. The least she could do was leave my workplace too. This is torture."

I was so appalled by this that I had to remind myself to close my jaw. "That's so inconsiderate. Isn't this her first year instructing the band? I've never even seen her until this year. What a wicked move. Oh. My. God. I bet she's staying because she wants to go with us to Disney . . . " I trailed off, having noticed the way I had started rambling and speaking out of turn. It certainly was not my place to question an adult's decision, let alone a staff member at the school, but at that moment I hated her. I hated her for what she did to you. It was at this moment that I realized I would have risked a lot more than speaking out of turn for you.

Your sad laugh pulled me back from my thoughts. "You are fiercely loyal, but I won't ask you to take a side here. You don't need to be upset on my behalf."

"I know and I will try harder to hide it, but I am angry for you. This is just . . . very unfair to you," I said softly.

My phone buzzed in my lap, a text from my mom asking if I would be home for dinner. I tried to ignore it, but you noticed.

You glanced at the clock and sighed. "I should go . . . and you should too. We shouldn't be alone, anyway." You ran a hand down your face in defeat.

I felt a rush at the implication of your words and the color of my cheeks deepened with embarrassment. "Oh! I'm so sorry, I shouldn't have stayed. I'll go now." I was flustered as I gathered my things quickly with shaking hands.

I stood and reached to get my folder, which I had left on the top of the piano. Your hand flickered past mine with a brief brush, momentarily rendering me immobile. "Don't apologize. I'm thankful you did." You paused, your eyes locked into mine. "It helps to have one of you know," you said. The sincerity in your eyes calmed my nerves and I felt my cheeks warm at your words.

"Of course," I smiled. "You have always been here for me, and I would like to return that favor to you if I can."

For the first time in a while, the smile that spread across your face appeared to be sincere. "Thank you. Please just . . . don't tell your peers? I will tell them eventually. I'm just not ready. I need to be a bit steadier before I open this up to their reactions."

I was deeply aware of the way your hand hovered, not far from mine. I nodded, softer this time. "I understand. I won't say a word."

"Thank you," you said again, with a quick tap of your knuckle on the back of my hand.

You leaned back and I slid my folder into my backpack. I pulled the strap over my shoulder and walked toward the door. You followed me, silent as we made our way to the threshold of your room. I took a step through the doorway and turned back to catch your eyes. "Good night, Davis," I said quietly, hoping not to call attention to the fact that I was leaving your room alone.

"Good night, kid." You smiled warmly, leaning against the doorframe.

I drove home and spent the evening thinking of you.

Over the months that followed this interaction, the intimacy between us grew, nurtured by the bond of secrecy. I felt more aware of every look you sent my way. I noticed the way I became the target of your winks, whispered words, and inside jokes. It felt involuntary, the way I would linger after class for a chance to catch you alone. It wasn't that I expected anything nefarious from you. I never believed you to be capable of allowing anything inappropriate. I simply hoped to ask how you were, to make you smile again, and to perhaps receive validation that my presence was one in which you found peace.

I think you did—find peace in my presence, that is. I kept my word, too. Well, almost. The only soul I told about your split was Maverick, who simply said, "That explains a lot."

At Christmastime, you told me that you had been feeling lonely. Of course this year hit especially hard. I listened as you shared this. I went home and told my mom about your struggles. We nearly invited you into our family that year. My mom and I cannot seem to help ourselves from nursing the wounded.

Instead, I planned a special gift for you. I invited the a cappella group to my house where we made a set of gingerbread cookies. I never told them why I felt we should do this for you and they never asked. We decorated each carefully, lining our hair and clothes with wisps of icing. When we finished we had a full set of little gingerbread singers that looked, more or less, like us. I laid them all on a tray with the one we had made to look like you, complete with waves of dark hair, thick framed glasses, and your favorite plaid shirt. You kept that one in a box on your desk.

Before we went to Disney, you finally addressed the choir. You told them all how you and your wife—Miss Cathy as some knew her—were separating. Your speech was calculated and you shared your news professionally, without any animosity or emotion at all. When the students asked, you informed them that "yes, she would be on the Disney Trip" and "no, this was not something that worried you." I, of course, knew better.

Several years after you had left my life, I sat on a plush couch across from my therapist. I had told her about my "general" anxiety and how it manifests in my dreams. This one had happened to be about you, again. I was back in high school, but you acted as if I weren't there, as if I had become a ghost to you. It was deeply upsetting.

She sat back and asked, "Can you tell me about your relationship with that teacher?"

I started slowly, explaining who you had been to me. "I had a little crush on my teacher," "He was just very kind and attentive," "In college . . . "

She was not pleased with this shortened version of our story. "Tell me more about high school."

I thought it was irrelevant. After all, you had never hurt me in high school. In my mind, you had never crossed a line or asked me for anything I wasn't willing to give. "Well, he went through a divorce my senior year and that was really hard on him."

She scribbled something in her notebook. Without looking up, she asked, "And how did you know that?"

I chewed on my lip for a moment, considering my response. Ultimately, I decided that I was paying her enough to warrant the truth. "He told everyone, eventually. He had to because she worked at the school . . . but he told me first."

At this, she stopped writing. "Told you first?" she asked.

I shrugged, "Yeah. He told me one day after rehearsal and asked me to keep it between us because he wasn't ready to share it openly. If it means anything, I asked."

She leaned over the notebook in her lap, capturing me with her eyes. What she said next changed my life, for better or worse. I am still deciding. "That was very unfair of him to burden you with his secrets. Have you ever heard of grooming?"

Thus marked the beginning of a very long journey to uncovering the truth about my relationship with you. A truth that, like the sun, burns to look at directly. This truth has turned my own memories against me. The truth is deeply frustrating and painful because our history runs through a foundational time in my life.

Several hours deep into therapy, I could finally admit that you put me in a position that was both unfair and damaging. I'm sure it was easy for you to unload your secrets to me. I was vulnerable and trusting, as a student should be with her teacher. This line you crossed probably felt harmless to you. I'm sure you did not consider what it could do to my seventeen-year-old mind. You didn't consider the way this would deepen my devotion to you or how this act would further isolate me from my unknowing peers. There are many who will label this behavior as calculated, a move meant to pull me under your power. Instead, I see a broken man who was selfish and reckless with me. Unfortunately, your intentions do not matter. Both narratives yield the same result.

Of course, if this had been only a reckless mistake, perhaps you would have realized this and left me alone three years later. Instead, you capitalized on my devotion to you and used this as a catalyst for your pursuit.

20

Just Friends

"We have talked about obstacles or roadblocks that might be in the way of us being anything other than just friends."

College—Year Two

Y ou once told me I made you feel young because we would talk late into the night. I hated it. Talking late into the night, that is. There is an old saying, "Nothing good ever happens after 2 a.m." Okay, not an old saying so much as a quote from *How I Met Your Mother*, but I think it's true nonetheless. It is for this reason, and my general love for sleeping during the hours of darkness, that I find myself longing for my bed by 9 p.m. most nights.

Staying on the phone with you in those late night hours was difficult, even as a college student. Out of respect for my roommate, I would walk down the hall in search of a study room. One night in late February, I had done exactly this. I was laying across a couple of hard chairs watching out the window as a brutal wind whipped through the campus. We had talked about, well, everything. What you had done that day, the astronomy test I nearly failed, and your plans for the a cappella group you hoped to start at your new school. There was a lull in conversation, which I filled with a sleepy yawn. After a beat of silence, you spoke, wistfully. "I really enjoy talking to you, Mary Beth. Maybe more than anyone else right now."

"I enjoy talking to you too." I smiled, once again alight by your favor.

"Do you . . . have you told anyone? About our . . . friendship?" Each pause stretched, as you searched for the words. I understood.

"I have." I was apprehensive, but always honest with you. I bit at my cuticles, worried you may have preferred my discretion.

"Good. I'm glad you have. I have too."

"You have?" I sat up in my seat.

"Do you remember how I talked about the guy who brought me back to church?" You didn't wait for my response. "Well, he is the pastor. I've been starting to feel like this . . . relationship with you might be headed somewhere. I want to be so careful. I want to make sure I'm not just following the desires of my flesh. I want to care for you and your heart. So, I asked him out to coffee."

I sucked in a breath. Every tiny confession you gave me was like a treasure pulled from the earth. I tucked each one safely into the back of my mind. *You care for my heart. You see this relationship going somewhere.* I always wanted so much more. Now, I wish you had given me less.

Before I could form an answer, you continued. "Anyway, we talked for hours. I told him about you. About our history. And then I asked for his advice. He advised me to proceed with caution, and I assured him that I intend to. Ultimately, he reminded me of something very important. We are not bound to the expectations of the world, but to those of God. As long as we are following Him, I think we are in good hands."

Another pause, filled only by my shaky breaths. I didn't recall rising from my chair, but I was pacing in circles around the small room.

Again, before I could speak, you continued. This time with a question. "What about you? What kind of guidance have you received about me?"

"Oh, nothing different really. My friends think the same thing, and ultimately, they trust me to follow where God leads."

"Good. I'm so glad we have people in our lives who can support us. If we take this path . . . if I call you my girlfriend—which I would really love to do—we will not always be met with the same grace.

We might lose friends. Some relationships may never recover. Is all of this something you are ready for?"

I felt untethered. I was floating somewhere above, watching as my teenage heart weighed the potential consequences of our choices. Your sigh pulled me back down to earth.

"I think so," I started. "I . . . I think anyone who is not willing to accept us is someone I don't want as a friend. You're more important to me than any of that."

"I think that is a good place to start. It's probably a bit different for me. People will offer a lot of grace for you. You have to understand, I have a lot to lose here."

I nearly dropped my phone. "Oh, I would never want that. I would never ask you to do that. We wouldn't have to tell anyone, if that would make it better. You can walk away from this now, and I will never tell anyone else. I promise. I just . . . "

You interrupted my rambling, with the confident voice of someone who had made his decision. "If I choose this, with you, I want you to know it will be because I have considered the consequences. I would never ask that of you. I need you to know that."

"Okay." I took a breath and decided to ask the question that was pressing into my skull so bad it almost hurt. "And do you think you are? Willing to take that chance for me?"

"I am," you confessed. "God, I wish I could see you right now, or just hold your hand." After a pause, you added, "Can I say that?"

"You can, and I feel the same way," I said, sinking back into my chair.

"What do you think your parents would say? I know their opinions are very important to you."

"I think they'd trust me." I shrugged. "I think they trust you too."

"I'm glad."

There was another stretch of silence as I took in your words. I had an odd urge to thank you, as if you had granted me a wish.

Finally, you spoke. "The only hesitation I have is the distance between us. I think we need to experience each other in person, don't you? I would rather take this step with you, hand in hand. Literally, I mean."

I laughed, though it felt inexplicably heavy. "I do. What do we do then? I don't see that changing any time soon. Unless you are moving back home?"

"Well, no, I'm not. But I am coming home for the summer. Are you?"

"I am," I smiled.

"Well, there we have it. Let's continue to grow this friendship and plan to spend as much time as possible together when I'm home. I want to be the one to tell your parents too. I think it needs to come from me. What do you think?"

I thought you were wonderful. I thought you were charming and thoughtful. I thought this was perhaps the most romantic thing to happen to anyone, and it was happening to me. I thought you were my dream come true. I wasn't entirely wrong, though the dream was much more haunting than I knew.

We moved forward from this conversation with intention. Nothing really changed and everything changed. You started taking chances with expressing desires to touch me and establishing boundaries that may have helped us avoid a lustful stumble if we were to end up alone together (something you referred to as a "conundrum"—this battle between desire and sin). You shared articles with me about Christian dating and sex, and I responded with my thoughts on the topics.

I do not pretend to understand the fine line between friendship and what we call, "more than friendship." I am inclined to suggest it might just be the desire for more, physically. Regardless, I am astonished that you believed we were ever friends. It makes me wonder about your idea of friendship. I imagine you talking about me with others referring to me as, "my friend, Mary Beth." It is laughable, really. I was a student, then a former student, and I fully believe you only referred to me as such. I would love a chance to ask you when exactly I was your friend.

Allow me to say it once more. We were never just anything. In fact, my relationship with you was anything but *just.*

21
Forgotten

"I think of you daily."

For many years you lived far away, but recently I learned you moved back home. Now, everywhere I go, I look for you. I am at the grocery store, selecting my produce, when I catch a glimpse of you. You're carefully examining an apple. Your hair is peppered in shades of gray and white but otherwise you look the same. I snap up, my body initiating fight or flight. I consider running away, hoping you haven't noticed me yet. I realize that if I did, I may never have a chance to speak to you again. I muster the courage to approach you just as your wife turns the corner, an arm full of various greens. She kisses you on the cheek as she sets them in the cart. I start to turn away, but you call my name. I walk to you, reluctantly. I start to respond, to call you by name, but I realize I am not sure what name to use. Tears threaten to spill at the realization, and I am shocked to find you do not seem to notice. You claim it's good to see me again, and I say the same, though I am not sure if I mean it. You carry on small talk as if this is normal, as if you hadn't told me about your desires and your demons when I was a child. I am hurt.

I awaken and wonder if you have forgotten about what you did to me or if you think so little of it that it has become irrelevant. I am not sure which is worse.

22

On My Own (Part 3)

"Your heart and its contents mean the world to me."

Twelfth Grade

I walked into the choir room one day in late October to a group of teens buzzing with excitement. I found Maverick and made my way to him. "What's going on?" I asked, scanning the room for you.

"Davis is going to announce what we will be singing at Disney this year!" He sang, grabbing my hands.

Our choir had been invited to travel to Disney this year with the band. We were all incredibly excited, even though we would not be going until March. As Maverick and I dove into the spiral of guesses about what we would get to perform, you waltzed into the room. Your arms were overflowing with what appeared to be packets of sheet music. "Oooooh, I think I see it. It's definitely *Lion King*," Maverick snickered.

I squeezed his hand excitedly before letting go to make my way back to my assigned section on the risers. You hushed the class and prepared us for the announcement.

"Hey you guys, what's all the excitement about?" you asked, with a sly smile.

"Cease with your antics, man!" yelled a bass from the top of the risers. At this, the class started to spiral into excited chatter once again.

You let this continue long enough that I became frustrated and started to shush my peers. Of course, it made no difference. I was prone to forget that I was one of them.

Finally, after several minutes you started to speak. "Alright, I guess you want to know . . . " You paused dramatically and the noisy teens settled into anticipatory silence.

"As you know, we are headed to Disney this year—shhh, that part is not new!" You snapped at the sopranos who had started to cheer. Once they had quieted back down, you shook your head and continued. "Anyway, you know we are set to perform at Universal Studios on the final day of our trip. I have selected a medley from a Broadway show . . . "

My heart jumped at the word Broadway, and I leaned forward in my seat. My breath caught in my chest when your eyes found mine. The smile reached your eyes, and for a moment we were the only two in the room. "Go on," I urged.

Your eyes stayed locked on mine as you continued. "I wanted to pick a medley that showcased the history of another country. France to be exact." At this, you gave me a knowing wink.

I nearly jumped out of my seat. "Oh my God. It's *Les Mis!*" I shouted, before I could remind myself to remain calm.

Instead of scolding my outburst, you bit back a smile and tapped your nose. "It is," you confirmed, as if you had been speaking only to me the whole time.

A few class members cheered, but most sat in silence. As it turns out, *Les Misérables* was not an incredibly popular or accessible choice for a group of teenagers. But I was beyond thrilled. It felt personal, like maybe you had me in mind when you made your selection. I tried to shake that thought away, knowing it was foolish.

A week or so later, you held auditions for the solos of the medley. Though every choice for a female solo would have been a good one, we all knew which one was mine. In class my fellow altos would joke, "We can audition for any part we want, but Eponine is Mary

Beth's. Don't even bother with that one." At least, I thought they were joking.

The day of auditions, not one of the girls in my audition group volunteered to rival me for Eponine. Though I was admittedly happy to secure the spot, I hated the idea that I would not have a chance to earn it, so I encouraged them to try for it as well. Then, I proceeded to audition for every single solo in the medley. However, I was sure to remind you in no uncertain terms, my heart was set.

Even though I may have been better suited for the ingenue, Cosette, you played into my fantasy and cast me as Eponine. I think you enjoyed this. Playing into my fantasies, I mean. I am noticing that you did this often. Was it thrilling for you to watch me glow? It's not that I am ungrateful or even that I wish you hadn't. These were some of the greatest moments of my youth. I just cannot help but notice a pattern.

23
Honor Choir

"As our relationship, friendship, continues to grow, so does my joy."

Twelfth Grade

When I was your student, I called you my favorite teacher. I have so many memories that now take multiple forms. In one version of each story, you are a teacher who goes above and beyond for his students. In this version you are an exceptional mentor who immerses himself in the experiences of his students in order to see them reach their full potential. You are a leader who sacrifices weekends, evenings, and so much energy to ensure we have the best experience possible while seeking out opportunities for us to grow our talents within and beyond your classroom. You were always directing me and guiding me to these new experiences that would give me a chance to develop as a performer.

My senior year, you encouraged me to audition for one of the regional honor choirs in our area. Honor choir was an annual weekend event where a select group of students would rehearse all day Saturday and Sunday for a performance Sunday evening. In my years as your student, I attended several of these. While some included a group of students hand-selected by their directors, others were by audition only. This one in particular was the auditioned type and of the handful of your students who auditioned,

I was the only one who was accepted. I was incredibly proud of myself for this, but also apprehensive about going into the weekend without my peers.

I walked into the unfamiliar high school and was immediately overwhelmed by the sheer size of the building. The entryway alone was the size of our football field. Vaulted ceilings made the space feel exceptionally large. Early morning sunlight lit the room, streaming in through the windows, which comprised the entirety of the wall. It all felt very grand. Coming from our small town, it was always a bit shocking to find that some schools were built to accommodate so many students. I felt out of place and jealous that our humble school did not have access to a space like this for the arts. While the other singers buzzed, screaming as they ran to their friends, I tried to stay out of the way. I tucked myself against the wall of windows on the outside of the room. As I anxiously scanned the sea of overexcited teenagers for a familiar face, I found you.

You gave me a warm smile and nodded, as you made your way through the crowd to me. I hadn't expected you to be there, and you acknowledged as much saying, "I didn't want you to be alone." My heart glowed as you told me about your plan to introduce me to the director and to stick around long enough to be sure I was comfortable.

"You didn't have to come. I know it is a long drive . . . but I'm glad you did," I said, as we walked into the auditorium.

We sat together, you turned around in the row in front of me with your arm casually draped across the chairs. We talked about our upcoming Disney trip. I was incredibly excited, but you were filled with dread. That's when you admitted your apprehension about your soon-to-be ex-wife who would be attending the trip.

I was devastated for you. "I'm so sorry," I remember saying. "I still can't believe she would do that to you." After all, this was the first year she had ever been involved in extracurriculars at our school. It seemed simple enough to decline attendance out of respect for her ex, who had been a full-time teacher with the school for nearly ten years. In my young mind, it was simple. I had thought the choir director was more necessary than her position anyway. But really, it was just because it was you. You won every time in my eyes, and like you had said before, I was fiercely loyal. I was loyal to a fault.

You agreed and told me that you had asked and that she had refused. That filled me with rage. "What are you going to do?" I asked, unsure how you would continue to hide the split from my peers while facing the forced proximity of five days together traveling and chaperoning a bunch of nosy teens.

You sighed, resigned to your fate. "I am going to tell everyone this week."

I saw the hurt, the worry, and the anger written in every feature of your face. I watched your fingers drumming anxiously and resisted the urge to press my hand over yours. I wanted to protect you from this, but I didn't know how I could.

It's a formative experience, watching your mentor crumble in front of you. I felt simultaneously honored that you continued to trust me with your feelings and frustrated that I couldn't be the friend you clearly needed.

As if you read my mind, you let a slow smile spread across your face. "I'll be okay," you assured me. "I just don't know what I would do without you . . . all of you. I am just grateful you all will be there to keep me distracted."

I know now what you meant, that the distraction of your job and my peers was enough to get you through. In fact, when my personal life would be troublesome in my adult years, I too found escape in my job and my students. The carefree nature of a child is a great escape for us adults.

However, I was seventeen and crushing hard on my teacher. All I heard then was that you didn't know what you would do without me. I heard that I was special, that your relationship with me was important to you, and that you needed me. Whether or not you intended to do so, you made me feel like maybe I was your friend after all. I am not alleging that you meant to, but rather letting you know that you did.

Later that day, after hours of rehearsing, I emerged from the auditorium in a sea of loud teenagers headed for the cafeteria. You were there, sitting at a high table across the hall. I smiled as you held up a finger, telling me to wait for you. Suddenly, I didn't care that not a single person asked for my name in rehearsal or invited me to sit with their group at lunch. It didn't matter so much that I didn't know how to interact with my fellow singers because you were there.

You stuffed your things into your shoulder bag and shuffled your way through the crowds of students.

"How was the rehearsal? Did you make any new friends?" you asked, aware that I was very much alone.

"Not really," I shrugged. "Everyone was very focused. It was actually really nice."

You laughed at that. "Want company for lunch? I was going to head out but thought you might not want to sit alone."

I accepted, of course, and you showed me the way to the cafeteria. I sat down and pulled out my packed lunch. My appetite vanished as I realized you would not be eating with me. I forced myself to nibble at my PB&J, and you talked.

That meal used to be one of my favorite memories. We talked about what I wanted to do after high school and whether I would be fulfilled pursuing a career outside of music and performance. You told me about your journey through college and gave me hope that I would find my place there. You said I reminded you a lot of yourself when you were younger. I didn't want that time with you to end. I soaked up every moment, and by the time you walked me back to the choir room for rehearsal, I had almost forgotten why I was there.

"I'll check in with you again tomorrow," you said, placing a hand on my shoulder. I made my way back into the classroom with renewed confidence.

When I went home that evening, I didn't think about all that I learned in that rehearsal. I didn't review my music or attempt to remember the new faces I spent hours with that day. Instead, I dwelled on every little moment you had chosen to spend with me. I knew you had traveled at least an hour, likely more, to spend that time with me. I replayed your words to me in the auditorium and felt a surge of warmth at the idea that you felt comforted by me. I shut my eyes and replayed the way your eyes crinkled when you laughed until the image was etched into my brain. I convinced myself that you didn't stay for lunch because I needed you, but because you wanted to. I tried my very best to memorize the feel of your hand on my shoulder, locking the feeling away in a corner of my mind that I saved just for you.

Whether this memory is twisted by what happened later is hard for me to discern. There is a version of this story where you are just an exceptional teacher who takes an interest in each of his students. But over time lines drawn in the sand were erased and moved so many times, I can't recall where we left them or when we decided they didn't apply to us anymore.

You see, this may have been an entirely appropriate exchange between a student and her director, or it was a moment of weakness and the boundary was blurred. Perhaps you could sense my devotion to you and it felt really good to know someone would be unquestionably on your side. Maybe you saw the way I looked at you and realized how much you craved being wanted. It could be that leaning into my feelings that morning rewarded you with the sense that you weren't alone, so you stayed close. The risk of appearing overinvested may have been worth it, because the alternative was to go home and face your loneliness.

I'm sure it appeared harmless to let yourself lean into my obsession with you, but I really wish you had kept your eye on that line in the sand, especially when the tide threatened its existence.

24
Beautiful

"You are a radiant beauty and you shouldn't be ashamed of that."

College—Year One (Almost)

I come from a family of wine enthusiasts. To some that may imply that my family drinks a lot, but that is not what I mean by this. What I intend to express is that my father is incredibly educated in the finest details of wine, a skill set that I now benefit from as a wine enthusiast myself.

When I was younger, my parents hosted several wine tastings at our house. My parents required weeks to prepare for these events. My mom would spend time cleaning and decorating the wine cellar, while my Dad poured into research. By the date of the party there would be printed binders for guests to read about the wines and a curated menu designed to pair each wine perfectly.

On the night of this party in June 2013, I was freshly graduated from high school and excited to spend an evening eating junk food and watching movies in my bedroom with my younger brother, Kyle. We had found early on that it was best to hide away during these events, unless we enjoyed receiving unsolicited advice from our parents' tipsy friends. Sometimes we would be joined by the other children of the friend group, and we would all hunker down in our rooms while our parents socialized downstairs.

That afternoon, about an hour before the tasting, Kyle and I sat at the bar in our kitchen. We were munching on chips that had been set out for the party and making plans for our night. My mom was buzzing around the kitchen, preparing the food as my dad assembled his binders.

"Will Sophia and Lydia be coming tonight, Mom?" Kyle asked through a mouth full of chips.

"I'm not sure, honey. Their dad is coming though. I am sure they would come hang out with you guys." She tossed the salad. "Miss Nancy is coming too. I told her Molly is more than welcome, MB."

"Oh cool. Yeah, I'll text her," I said, plucking a grape off of a bunch. "Anyone else?"

"Hmm, well, Megan and Liam's mom and dad will be here, but the kids are with their grandparents in Michigan. Other than that I can't think of anyone you would want to spend time with." Mom was putting the salad in the fridge. She turned her head over her shoulder, "Oh! And Mr. Davis is coming I think. Nancy asked if we could invite him. Sounds like he's been going through it lately and could use a night out."

My stomach dropped, a wave of suspense hitting as I forced myself to swallow my grape. "Mr. Davis is coming to our house?" I asked, hesitantly.

"Yeah, shoot. Is that okay, sweetie? I can say no!"

My brother and I exchanged a look. Our mother was capable of many things, but saying no was not one of them. This was especially true if she learned somebody was feeling lonely or sad. Anyway, I didn't want her to decline. I was thrilled, if a little anxious, at the intimacy of having you in my home.

"You ready to go, sis?" Kyle asked, sliding out of his seat as he snagged another handful of chips.

"Uh, yeah, just . . . give me a second. I need to change." I started toward the stairs, already itching to change out of my pajama pants.

"What? Why can't you wear what you already have on? You're so ridiculous!" called Kyle, clearly annoyed.

I ignored him, sprinting to my room. I pulled on jeans first but decided I looked too obviously dressed up and worried you might notice that I dressed for you. After several more attempts at capturing effortlessly cute, I ended up settling on a pair of lounge shorts and a black tank. I let my hair down and shook the curls, hoping they would choose to play nice for me. With a delicate mixture of curl cream, hairspray, and bobby pins, I twisted them into submission. I threw on a bit of makeup, focusing on blurring my most recent breakout. At last, when I was content, I walked back downstairs, as if taking time to get ready for a night locked in my bedroom was normal.

"Ready!" I proclaimed as my brother rolled his eyes. I grabbed my keys and pushed Kyle out the door, wanting to be back home before you arrived.

I drove my brother down to our local grocery store. Together we picked out the junkiest of snacks and shuffled over to the Redbox machine, arms overflowing with processed sugars. I started flipping through the movies, and we made our selection. As I finished the process of checking out our movie, I sent Kyle to purchase our snacks, with a plan to meet at the front of the store. The machine was finicky, and I had a hard time getting my card to process. As I continued fighting the machine, a man approached from behind. At first I ignored him, assuming he was just waiting for his turn. However, moments later he crept closer and I was engulfed in the discomfort of his proximity.

"Oh, nice choice. I was going for that one too. Maybe I should just come over and watch it with you?" he said, his tone far too flirtatious to be appropriate.

Chills ran down my spine as the machine spit out my disk. I snatched the DVD and turned, nearly knocking the man over as I speed-stepped to my brother.

"Ew, Kyle, get in the car. We have to leave. Now. That man over there is so creepy," I whispered.

On the drive home I tried to brush off the whole interaction. Instead, I contemplated how I would react to you, wondering whether feigning surprise at your presence or acting nonchalant would be a better approach. My heart jumped with anticipation as we pulled into the long driveway. I let out a sigh, whether in relief or disappointment I can't be sure, when I determined that your car was nowhere in sight.

Kyle and I shuffled through the guests in the kitchen as we made our way upstairs to burrow in for our first movie. Our friends had agreed to hang with us, but they would not be arriving for another hour or two. Kyle and I ate Twizzlers and Hershey's Kisses and laughed our way through whatever absurd movie we had selected. Though I attempted to relax, I spent the whole time plotting an excuse to come see you.

When the movie ended, we decided to make popcorn, which to my delight required a trip to the kitchen. Immediately, I scanned the room. I saw a few of my parents' friends mingling, their glasses full of a California red, but no sign of you.

"Hey, MB! Kathryn just texted. They are headed over and should be here soon," Kyle said from across the room, placing the bag of popcorn in the microwave. "Should we play that new game we got?"

"Sure!" I exclaimed, as I did a second sweep of the room. If you were here, you must have made your way into the wine cellar. "Hey, I am going to go find Mom! I'll be back in a second," I told Kyle, slipping away and heading for the stairs.

I found you there at the bottom of the stairs, chatting at the high top with a glass in your hand. You were sitting across from my mom, laughing with her. I came over and leaned on the table next to you, deciding at that moment that I needed to tell my mom about my encounter at the grocery store.

My mom turned to me and immediately wanted to know if I was okay. "Do you need something, sweetie?" she asked, sipping what was definitely not her first glass.

"No, we are all good. Kyle's just making popcorn." She relaxed, bringing her nearly empty glass to her lips. "But Mom. Listen to what happened at the Redbox!" I leaned in, emphasizing the drama of my tale. "Some old man came up to me and said he wanted to come over and watch a movie with me," I said, wrinkling my nose in disgust.

My sweet, anxious mother was appalled. "What? He didn't follow you, did he? Why would he say that?" She was clearly starting to spiral, and I immediately regretted my choice to share. I should have anticipated her reaction.

You, however, remained unbothered. You laughed, shifting your body to face me. "That's not surprising. Of course he was hitting on you. Look at you. You are a beautiful young woman."

Time stood still, or at least I did. I was frozen, my mind repeating on an endless loop, *he just called me beautiful.*

Whether in the name of honesty or alcohol, you chose to expand upon this thought.

"No really!" you exclaimed, as if being shocked at your blatantly inappropriate remark was unwarranted. You turned, addressing my mom directly now, "Listen. If I wasn't her teacher . . . Well, I guess I'm not anymore, huh?" you paused, turning your eyes to meet mine. You winked and turned back to continue. "Anyway, if I never had been, would it be weird to you? If I was hitting on your daughter?"

I put my hand over my mouth as nervous laughter escaped me. I attempted to regain composure, my mind searching for the intention behind your question. Was this some kind of confession that you wished you could hit on me openly? My brain tried to save me, suggesting that you were just trying to make me feel less uncomfortable about the whole interaction. Yet, somewhere in the swarm of thoughts I heard the echo—*beautiful young woman.*

Never one to seek confrontation, my mom laughed awkwardly, punctuating the discomfort between us. Before she could speak, someone approached with an empty glass and a question about the next tasting. Relief flooded her expression, as she found an excuse to dodge this uncomfortable question. "Oh, yes! Let's head upstairs, Jeff has a little background prepared for this next one, and you all know he would be disappointed if we missed it!"

You showed no intention to follow and I was drawn to stay, hoping you hadn't reached the end of your boozy confessions. I longed for more information about your feelings. For the sake of my sanity, I needed more to grasp when this night was over than the little words that echoed in my mind. *Beautiful young woman.*

With most of our audience gone, you crossed your legs and leaned casually on the table. "How are you feeling, kiddo? Big changes ahead for you." You lifted your cup only to find it was empty.

"I'm nervous, but excited. Feeling a little anxious about living in a dorm, honestly." I sat on the stool next to you, solidifying my decision to stay here as long as you would allow.

"Makes sense, it can be intimidating, especially if you don't know anyone. Don't worry though; everyone will love you. What's not to love?"

I blushed. "Yeah, well, I am just not good at making new friends. Luckily I do know my roommate though. Well, kinda. We found each other on the Facebook page for new students and have been texting a bit. She's really nice, but she makes me feel a little worried, too."

"Why's that?" you asked, grabbing a glass of wine from my dad, who was passing around the next red on his list to those who did not attend his tutoring session upstairs.

"We just don't have anything in common. She isn't really into performance, she doesn't know any musicals, and she's a runner," I said, crinkling my nose at the repelling thought of voluntary cardio. "She's super skinny and blond and pretty . . . " I trailed off, unsure whether I should have made my insecurities so clear to you.

"Well, skinny and blond does not mean she's pretty. Let me see her." Your hand reached for me, indicating that I was to give you my phone.

I am not sure why, but I didn't hesitate to pull out my phone and swipe into her Facebook profile for you. I did so quickly, noting her beautiful face as I passed my phone to you, our hands brushing in the exchange.

You took a long look, even swiped through a few of her photos, before responding. "Eh, she's not *that* pretty. She looks old, don't you think?" You shrugged, as if this was an obvious observation.

I leaned in for a closer look and found myself enveloped in the familiar scent of your cologne. I analyzed her profile picture. I saw her blond waves, falling over her tan shoulders, and tried to see what you could possibly mean by that. Like me, she was seventeen, and admittedly I thought she looked it.

We sat like that, talking about my college roommate and strategizing how I would select which choir I would add to my schedule until someone interrupted us, inviting you to the patio for a cigar. Resigned, I followed you up the stairs and joined my friends on the couch. They had progressed into the living room as the adults made their way outside.

Much later in the evening, nearly everyone was gone, but you inexplicably remained. I could see your shadow through the back window, sipping bourbon with my dad. As the last of the guests trickled out, you stumbled inside. Your hands were full of broken glass and you were muttering an apology about breaking one of my dad's special whiskey glasses. I helped you discard the broken glass and assessed your hands for any injuries as my mother left to retrieve the broom. Once you were cleaned up, you wished me a good night and went out the door. I could hear the back and forth in the driveway when my dad suggested you couldn't drive home. After an internal debate, I came outside and offered to drive you myself. I was the only sober one with a license, after all, and it was a short drive. You insisted you would make it up the street and got into your car before I could protest. I watched you drive away, filled with anxiety that you'd make your way into a ditch somehow. With no way to determine whether you had arrived home safely, I eventually padded upstairs and went to sleep.

The next morning I woke from a restless sleep, having stayed awake most of the night attempting to decode your tipsy unbosoming. I rolled over, grabbed my phone from the charger, and typed a quick SOS message to Maverick. I spent the next several minutes lying in bed waiting for his response. When I couldn't lie still any longer, I slid out of bed and pulled on my shorts, determined a walk in the fresh air would clear the dizzying thoughts in my head.

As I walked, I analyzed the implications of your words. It was starting to feel like I wasn't entirely delusional for feeling that you saw me as special. It felt like dangerous territory to enter, knowing I was one to spiral. I wondered if you also fantasized about a different life where we met as equals, as I often had. I hoped you would continue this level of transparency with me now that I was not in your classes and the official line between teacher and student no longer applied to our relationship.

Finally, my phone buzzed with an incoming call from Maverick. Before I could even say hello, Maverick started spewing with anticipation, "Girl, what happened? Tell me now."

I laughed at his eagerness, letting myself relax into the safety of his friendship. "Okay, so you know how Davis came over last night? He said some things . . . " I began.

I recounted the details to him, being mindful not to embellish. I wanted him to provide his unbiased analysis, given only the facts. He laughed at my conclusion saying, "Yeah well, we all know he's in love with you. I'm disappointed he didn't say anything juicier." I smiled and welcomed his perspective, even if it was a bit overdramatic.

After this conversation, I vowed to keep your words to myself. I didn't want others tainting my memory by insisting you were spewing drunk nonsense. Those words lived, untouched, in my mind for many years, always drawing me to the same conclusion. *He thinks I am beautiful.*

My parents told stories of your unhinged behavior at their wine tasting for years to come. The way you said your most recent hookup played an April Fools' joke on you by telling you she was pregnant. The way you drove home and back to share your special bottle of bourbon. The glass you broke and the drunken determination to make it right. Lucky for you, no one remembers the way you tested the waters with me over a glass of wine. But I do.

I remember the earnest look on your face when you told me I was a beautiful young woman. I recall the way you pushed at the line, asking if I would be creeped out by the advances of a man fourteen years my senior. I remember that wink when you pointed out that I was no longer a student to you, a change that I had previously determined largely immaterial to our relationship.

As time has passed, this moment has become a pivotal one in our story. Whether a lack of judgment or an intentional choice, these words have served as a point of clear change in our relationship. For better or worse, I moved on from this day believing that you too wished for something that had been forbidden by circumstance.

Now that I'm grown, I see this for what it is. This was a grown man calling one seventeen-year-old "beautiful" and saying another was too "old" to be attractive. These were the words of a man who had continually favored me and treated me differently than my peers for nearly four years. This behavior was a part of a pattern, one that unfortunately is so common that it is clinically labeled. Whether intentional or accidental, this was grooming. That line in the sand between us had been eroding in time, and with it, I had forgotten my place.

I may have continued to believe in your innocence, if only you had left me alone after that night. In the other version of our story I sometimes write in my dreams, I can explain this away as the foolish behavior brought on by an overindulgence in loneliness and alcohol. However, that story faded into fiction and the pattern turned into something much less ambiguous and much more dangerous.

25
Closer

"I truly wish I was able to be closer to where you are . . ."

Twelfth Grade

Once again, I feel the need to highlight the way that you occupied nearly every corner of my life. I saw you for at least two hours every day during school, followed by hours every weeknight for show choir, the musical, and a cappella group rehearsals. Many weekends, I would see you at some point on Saturday, whether it was for set constructions, small group performances, honor choirs, or competitions. The only day I was nearly guaranteed to be without you was Sunday.

On Sundays, I spent the whole day at church. I would wake early for practice with the worship team. The team consisted of myself on vocals; my youth director, Brandon, on guitar; and Miss Nancy, who would harmonize and play piano. Making music with that team was one of my favorite parts of the week. It was an incredibly safe and encouraging space for me.

One Wednesday night in November, I showed up to my weekly church rehearsal after a long day. Due to my already packed schedule, we rehearsed at 7 p.m., after my school obligations were over. This particular night, I had pulled my curls into the messiest bun I could manage and slipped into sweatpants, nearly ready for bed. When I walked into the sanctuary, I heard someone strumming guitar and chatting. I froze, listening to confirm what I already knew.

"Yeah, well, I think I can probably sell this ring now and get myself a new guitar, don't you think?" said a voice, through a chuckle. Yup, that was definitely you.

I turned the corner into the sanctuary, tugging at my escaping curls, immediately becoming self-conscious about my disheveled appearance.

"There she is!" you proclaimed from behind your guitar. Your shoes were off, and you had your feet propped on the speaker in front of you, appearing incredibly casual in this new space.

"What is happening?" I said, giggling at the sight of your pink and blue mustache socks.

"I was just talking with Nancy at school, and she suggested I join you all here on Sundays. Is that okay?" you asked, sitting up to face me.

"Why wouldn't it be?" I laughed, as I set my things up at the microphone, laying my music out on my stand. It somehow made sense that you would be here in this space. It was my only musical outlet that was devoid of your presence and influence.

After that night, your residence in my life extended to weekly rehearsals and Sunday services. Every now and then, we would play at a youth event or a Saturday evening community dinner. As if I didn't feel close to you before, now I was given a look into a whole new version of you. This was you outside of school. At church you never acted very professionally, letting your guard down to a fault. These late nights in the sanctuary were where you let details about your personal life spill out.

One night at rehearsal, you were particularly on edge. You arrived agitated and appeared generally flustered. Your usually perfectly set hair was tousled, as if you had been running your hand through its waves.

"Hey, Mr. Davis," I said as you approached, "you okay?"

"Hey MB," you mumbled, placing a quick hand on the small of my back as you passed. The gesture meant to acknowledge my presence sent an electric shiver up my spine.

After running the first two songs, we took a quick break. On my way back from refilling my water bottle, I heard you talking with the other adults. There was a tone in your voice I had never heard before but recognized as anger.

"After seven years together, she can't even . . . " You paused as you noticed my presence, locking eyes with me across the room.

The other adults tried to change the subject, clearly flustered. You stopped them with a hand.

"It's okay. She already knows," you said, never taking those raging eyes off of me.

"I do." I nodded, tentatively coming to join you on the stage. I took my seat next to you as you filled us in on the most recent update to your personal life. You had to sell your home, leaving you to find a new place to live.

The other adults were quick to offer their help and possible solutions, as I sat quietly longing for something helpful to say. At seventeen, there was nothing I could offer you. I would have given you the guest room at our house if it was mine to offer. Hell, I would've given you my own room.

Instead, I listened. I listened the next week when you told the group how you were suspicious of her male friend.

One week I arrived a few minutes early for rehearsal. I opened the door to the church and heard the piano playing. As I walked down the hall, I could make out your voice. You were sitting at the keyboard, singing. I didn't recognize the song, but after more than four years with you, the tone of your voice was deeply familiar. I stopped walking immediately, not wanting your song to end on my account. Instead, I stood there, listening. At that moment, hearing you pour your heart into your music, drinking in the sound of your voice as it filled the room, I started to cry.

Your pain had been slowly infecting me through the year, and I was sick with your sadness. I ran to the church bathroom and locked myself in the stall, taking deep breaths and talking myself back down. This was not the first time that I had cried for you—it was a frighteningly regular occurrence. However, the last thing I wanted was for you to see it. I worried that if you knew how it made me feel, you would stop trusting me with your feelings.

When I returned, Nancy had arrived and taken her place at the piano, putting you back at your guitar. You smiled at me when I came onto the stage.

"There she is. How's it going, kiddo?" you asked, as if I hadn't seen you an hour earlier at rehearsal for the musical.

"I'm fine, just not feeling my best," I said honestly. The truth was that I had not yet learned to manage the monthly fire in my abdomen, and it burned with a promise to knock me off my feet as soon as I made it home.

That rehearsal was particularly difficult for me. I struggled to find the harmonies and was spiraling into a hormone-induced melt-down. Whenever I was upset with myself, I'd shut down, retreating into my own thoughts. Sometimes I would be completely unaware of those around me as I tried to quiet the internal monologue that offered unhelpful critiques and criticism. I'd often been told that I looked angry when this happened, and I guess that was true this time too.

Nancy must have noticed because she stopped playing and turned on the bench to face me. "Are you alright, Mary Beth? You seem frustrated."

Before I could answer, you looked up from behind your guitar. "She gets like this sometimes. She's just swirling around in that brain of hers. Don't worry, she'll figure it out."

I smiled at you, filled with the warmth of being known. "He's right. I was just processing . . . I do get like this a lot, don't I?"

"I've got an idea," you said. "You've got to shake this one off. Let's sing something you want to sing. No harmonies to learn, no stress about notes. I just want you to sing. I'll play for you. Just tell me the song."

I felt silly as I found myself answering your spontaneous proposal. "Well, I have always wanted to sing 'Only Hope' at church," I confessed, sure you would say to pick something more well known.

"Hmm, do I know it?" you asked, clearly unaware of the cinematic masterpiece that is *A Walk to Remember*.

I pulled out my phone and showed you my favorite scene from that movie, an angelic Mandy Moore singing a song ambiguous enough to be about either God or an all-consuming love.

After a few minutes of broken runs through the song, trying to get the chords, we did it. After our first run, you told me I sounded "lovely." I remember it exactly. You said my voice was simple and lovely. On the third run, you started to harmonize with me.

There is something so intimate about singing with somebody. It's such a sacred act, blending your voice with another. I had sung for you, you had sung for me, we had even sung together. But we had never sung like this. This was different.

Those nights spent together, singing and sharing in community, were the nights when it started to feel a bit more intentional, this blurring of our lines. It was if you were dipping your toe across that line in the sand, experimenting with the consequences before drawing it back. Maybe you weren't, and maybe I made this up in my mind because I wanted you to feel more for me than you felt for your other students, but I swear you joined my church because you felt it too.

26

On My Own (Part 4)

"(Your heart) has already poured into me and made me glad!"

Twelfth Grade

When we finally went to Disney in March of my senior year, we spent our first day in Hollywood Studios. We stood, gathered in a cluster outside of the gates, waiting to receive our groups. I was put into a group with a few of my very good friends to be chaperoned by . . . Cathy Davis. I felt nauseated at the announcement. I walked to her slowly, the weight of dread heavy in my stomach. I had never met her, in all these years as your student. I assume she had attended concerts, but she never lingered long enough for me to catch a glimpse.

Cathy was a pretty, brunette woman with a warm smile that spread as I approached her.

"Mary Beth, I am so glad to finally meet you. Will, I mean, Mr. Davis, has told me so much about you." I wanted to smack the smile off of her face. I nodded and she continued. "I know it's probably weird, being Davis's student but having me as a chaperone. It's okay, we can acknowledge that."

"It's not weird," I said, quickly. I did not want to be kind to her, and I felt oddly protective of my relationship with you, like it was something she wouldn't understand. Apparently I chose to make the awkward situation worse by continuing to speak. "Mrs. er, Davis? I'm sorry, what should we call you?"

"Cathy," she corrected me with that warm smile of hers. "You can just call me Cathy if it is okay with you."

I tried my best to hate her all day. I tried to remain stoic when she made what were admittedly funny jokes. I scowled when I saw the way my peers laughed along as though she had done nothing wrong. I had to remind myself that to them, she didn't. She complimented my singing, saying that she had heard me at my concerts and been told about my development as a performer. I blushed and muttered a small "thank you." The bigger compliment was knowing you had talked about me.

When we passed the auditions for the park's *American Idol*, Cathy nodded her head toward the entrance. "You should totally do that! I will take you if you want," she said, her voice sincere and encouraging.

After much debate, I had agreed to try. We waited in line and talked about what I would sing. Cathy suggested we call you to let you know I was auditioning. I declined. I would rather you did not have to speak to her on my account. Plus, I didn't want you to know if I failed. She must have decided to let you know anyway because as I stood in line, I received a message from you.

```
Heard you're auditioning! Good luck, break a leg,
you got this! — D
```

You always signed your texts, as if I had not saved your number by now.

```
Thanks! I'm so nervous.
```

I hit send and put my phone away. I auditioned and failed to make it past round one. The judge implied my voice was too musical theater, which I found to be a compliment. I brushed it off and chose to believe it was for the best. This way, I could enjoy the park.

Instead of singing through the park's competition, I spent the rest of the day trying desperately not to be charmed by the woman who I knew had hurt you. This, it turned out, was not an easy task. Cathy was kind, funny, and charismatic. She asked me about myself, and I learned more about her than I had intended.

That night, after we had all returned to our hotel rooms, I managed to negotiate the first shower among my group. When I emerged from the bathroom, hair wrapped in a towel, the three girls staying with me were gathered around a table. They snapped to look at me, faces filled with intrigue.

"What?" I said, looking down to confirm that I had put on my pajamas.

"Why did Mr. Davis text you?" Katie said, eyes wide.

I flushed and ran to snatch my phone from the group of curious girls. Thankfully, they had not figured out how to get past my lock screen. I sighed with relief as I swiped to open your message.

```
Sorry you didn't get past the audition! I heard you
killed it! I guess you're just too good at theater.
— D
```

I bit back a smile and shoved my phone in the pocket of my pajama shorts. "It's nothing. He just wanted to make sure we all made it back to the room." I shrugged, trying to hide the way your message made my heart buzz.

"Yeah, right. He was probably just hoping to catch you out past curfew," Lacy teased.

The next morning was our performance. The choir had been set up in the plaza of Epcot. It was a cloudy, unexpectedly chilly day in Florida. We had no coats to pair with our performance gowns and I shivered against the breeze. We had not been joined by our accompanist on this trip, so in his place a track started playing. I held my eyes on you as you cued our entrance. While we sang, crowds funneled by, flashing encouraging smiles. Some even stopped to watch and cheered with each transition. All the while, I never looked away from you.

When the time came for my solo, I stepped forward and took my place at the microphone, which had been set next to you. I centered myself with a deep breath as the melody shifted into the familiar, dreamy introduction of "On My Own."

I closed my eyes and threw myself into my character. Here, in Disney, singing under your direction for what I knew would be one of the last times, I could feel our time together was slipping away. It hit me like a hammer, driving the point deep into my veins. You were not forever.

Without me, his world will go on turning. The words echoed in my head as I sang and I felt the sting in my eyes. I realized that I was no more than a student to you, one who would graduate and move on in a few short months. Our relationship was not one that stretched beyond our circumstance, which was fleeting. I choked back the lump in my throat and forced myself to finish my solo.

When I turned to rejoin the choir, I found myself blinking through hot tears. Embarrassed, I buried my face in my music and shielded myself from your gaze until I was sure there was no trace of my tears. When I did, you were looking at me. "Good job," you mouthed, with a nod.

When I recall my trip to Disney, these are the moments I remember first. I should remember exploring the parks with my friends or eating at the themed restaurants. I should remember meeting princesses and dancing along to the parades. I do. It's just that those childlike moments are buried under my thoughts of you.

27

The First Goodbye

"Distance makes the heart grow fonder. I think there's truth to that."

College—Year One (Almost)

It was a beautiful Saturday afternoon in early July. The sun was bright, hot, and high in the sky. I was wearing my favorite sundress, a short white-laced thing with thin straps that tied into little bows on my shoulders. I pulled my sunglasses up onto my forehead, shoving my curls back, as I turned into the shady drive of your temporary home.

Every year after graduation, you would invite the new grads to your home for a barbeque. This was a highly anticipated event among your students because it was said that you used the opportunity to get candid. Over the years, you had promised answers to our burning questions saying only, "You can ask me that at your senior-Q."

"Ooooh pretty!" said Maverick, as we drove up the gravel road, which was flanked by evergreen trees.

Due to the circumstances of your personal life, this year the event could not be held at your home, per se. You had been living in a makeshift apartment on property owned by a colleague of yours. There was a quiet charm to this humble space out here in nature. It may have been a temporary solution, but I thought it suited you nonetheless.

We drove a ways through the trees before we approached a red barn at the back of the lot. As we pulled in, I noticed we had been first to arrive. I was nothing if not punctual, sometimes to a fault. Anticipation coursed through my veins. I hadn't seen you since that night at my house, and the memory hung there in my mind, taunting me. *He thinks I'm beautiful.*

We got out of the car, Maverick holding a jug of sweet tea and me with a tray of snickerdoodles I had made the night before. "Where do we go?" I asked Maverick. I looked around, searching for an open door. The barn was small and rustic. There was an opening in the middle, which seemed to lead directly through to the other side.

"I think we just go in there," Maverick said, pointing to the opening.

We walked in tentatively, scanning the space. To my right, there was a little door with a small glass window in the middle. I stole a peek inside the tiny room. I could see a bed, a dresser, and a little couch. The space looked simple, yet cozy. I found my eyes lingering, assessing the little details of decor that you had selected. You must have heard us enter because you came up through the other side of the barn. "Welcome to my home!" you said loudly, arms outstretched.

I smiled, taking in your casual summer clothes. You were dressed in a simple white T-shirt and light wash jeans. Though not exactly tanned, you had new freckles along your nose where the sunlight had left its mark. You closed the gap between us and noticed the cookies in my arms. "Oh, MB! I love your snickerdoodles!" you sang as you grabbed the tray from my hands. I blushed at the compliment and followed you into the back.

As we walked, Maverick noticed another car pulling into the drive, "Oh! I think that's Jake. BRB!" He skipped back, leaving us alone.

The back of the barn stretched on as a sort of covered patio. You had placed several folding chairs in a large circle. There were two tables set up at the back with bags of hamburger buns and plates. I scanned the porch, taking in every bit of this space you had claimed.

"It's not much, but it's been good to me," you said from behind me.

I turned to you and smiled sweetly. "I like it. It's simple. I think simple is good."

You nodded and gestured to the little kitchenette in the barn. "I will say, one major downside is that the kitchen isn't exactly shielded from the elements. I have had some frigid mornings out here."

I could picture you there, bundled up, cooking yourself a meal. I giggled at the thought.

You feigned hurt at my reaction. "Hey, you can't laugh until you've made your coffee out here in nothing but your winter coat." I laughed even harder at the image and you chuckled.

"Alright, you two, knock it off!" yelled Jake, cutting through our laughter. You turned to Jake, sending me a look through the sides of your eyes suggesting they'd never understand us. Another giggle escaped, and I put my hand over my mouth to hide my smile. You were so casual in this space. It made me a bit giddy.

The rest of the graduates arrived in a trickle, bearing various sides and drinks. You spent most of the time over at the grill while I chatted with Lacy and Katie.

"Oh my God, you guys. He is living in a barn," Lacy whispered, aghast.

"Ew, I know!" said Katie. "He definitely lost the breakup."

"Knock it off," I hissed. I felt unreasonably defensive of you.

"Why don't you two just kiss and get together already," Katie teased. Lacy rolled her eyes. She shoved a finger in her mouth and made a gagging motion.

"Whatever, just . . . be nice," I said, resigned.

Lacy gasped and pulled us in closer. "You guys! Look! Look at Davis's neck."

I swept my eyes over to where you stood at the grill. Your head was turned, talking to someone I couldn't see. What I did see was a little red splotch on your neck, just under your ear.

Katie gasped. "A hickey! Oh my God. He could have at least tried to hide it!"

Katie and Lacy burst into girlish giggles while a feeling like jealousy bubbled up inside of me. It was an incredibly embarrassing feeling. I rolled my eyes at myself, internally scolding my behavior. *Get a grip, girl. This man is not available. Not for you, anyway.*

Eventually, it was time to eat. We all loaded our plates with food and made our way to the circle of chairs. I had landed near the back of the line and found that most of the chairs had been taken. For whatever reason, the only chair that remained open was the one closest to you, like it had been saved for me. I sat in my chair and listened as you answered the questions that had been directed to you. Yes, you thought the school should have done better to prevent bullying. No, this teacher was not romantically involved with that teacher. Yes, it would appear that so-and-so might be gay, but no, they had never told you as much. It continued like this as we finished our meals. I put my empty plate on the floor between my legs and did my best to absorb every honest answer.

"Oh, oh! Have you ever had a student that had a crush on you?" Jake asked from his chair across the circle. I swiveled to look at you, my curiosity piqued by the question.

"I have. It was pretty uncomfortable actually," you admitted.

"Alright then, tell us the story!" Lacy pressed.

"Well, I was a bit younger, in my early twenties. There was a girl, I won't name names because there was a year of crossover for you all with this individual. At first, she would just flirt and leave me little notes on my desk. I knew it was just a schoolgirl crush. I thought it would fizzle naturally, as those things do. Eventually, she started leaving me gifts and asking me questions about my personal life. That's when I had to intervene. I sat her down and laid out the boundaries. No more gifts, no more flirting, and definitely no more conversations about my personal life. I haven't had a problem since." You shrugged, and the group propelled into theories about which upperclassman you had been talking about.

Not me, though. I wasn't curious about the identity of this mysterious girl. I was stuck on the things you said. If you noticed her schoolgirl crush, surely you had noticed mine, too. You discouraged her from having personal conversations with you, but you openly shared your life with me. I recognized immediately that I was the same as her, but also somehow different. I wanted to ask you why you never discouraged me. I needed to know what made me different from her. I wondered if it meant that maybe, possibly, the difference was that you liked me too. I shifted uncomfortably in my seat at that thought and asked if you had a restroom I could use. I needed some space.

"I do. But it's just the one and it's in my room. Here, I'll show you," you said, standing. You led me to your room, the one with the little glass window. You opened the door and gestured for me to enter first. I walked in and assessed the space. It was actually very charming. Your messenger bag hung on a hook by the door next to a navy raincoat. Your bed was made up with a dark blue comforter folded expertly at the bottom over matching sheets. There was no door on the nook that appeared to have been made into a make-shift closet, so your dress coats and shirts hung there in the open. A flannel blanket was draped along the back of the leather couch. Your guitar was sitting there next to the couch, as if you had been playing moments before. There was a small stack of books on the coffee table and the only mess worth noting was a half-finished coffee cup on the side table.

"It's humble," you said, watching me assess your room.

"It's nice," I replied, feeling a little breathless. "It's just, very . . . you."

You smiled, your head tilting to the side. "Anyway, the bathroom is behind that door there." You pointed to the only door on the other side of the room, turned, and left me there alone.

When I returned, the conversation in the circle had lulled. Someone had moved into my seat. I was a little annoyed but chose to go sit next to Maverick and Jake instead of asking for my spot back. I wouldn't dream of the confrontation.

Suddenly, you spoke up, loud enough to grab the attention of everyone in the space. "Hey, so I have an announcement that I need to make."

Everyone fell silent. What could you possibly have to tell a group of kids who were no longer your students?

"This all happened suddenly, but I have resigned." At this, I felt almost relieved. Of course, I was sad that you would be leaving a school where you had poured so much of yourself into building a program, but I was not surprised by this. We had talked about your discomfort working alongside your ex over the past year and your intent to apply to the surrounding districts. If anything, I was happy for you.

You paused as several students gasped. Your eyes searched the circle, as if looking for someone. You said this next part carefully, catching my eyes as you spoke. "I have accepted another position . . . in Portland, Oregon."

My stomach dropped. I felt sick. I wanted very much to turn away from you, but I couldn't. "When?" I mouthed, the words failing to come out completely.

"Two weeks," you answered.

At that moment, it felt like the floor had fallen away from me. My vision blurred with what I realized were tears threatening to escape. I stood and muttered some excuse about needing to run to my car. I walked quickly as hot tears burned my cheeks. I found a spot at the side of the barn that was secluded enough to let me cry without eliciting more teasing from my peers. It was such a shock. I wondered if I would ever see you again, and a sob caught in my throat at the thought. It's embarrassing how deeply hurt I was by this.

Suddenly, I heard footsteps in the grass behind me. I wiped at my face and choked down my sobs.

"Hey kid," you said. You put a hand on my shoulder and pulled me into a tender hug. I focused on steadying my breathing. I was ashamed of my emotional response. You pulled away and held a napkin out, "Sorry, I don't have any tissues."

I let out a sad laugh as I took the napkin from your hands. "Why did you wait so long to tell me . . . I mean us?" I asked, dabbing the tears from my face.

"I didn't. It all just happened very fast," you spoke slowly. "I knew this would upset you. I'm sorry that I didn't have a chance to prepare you."

"Upset? That I'll never get to see you again?" I laughed without humor. "Never mind how I feel. Why are you leaving? Why are you giving up everything you have worked to build here? Your whole life is here! Why are you letting her take that from you?" I was a bit hysterical now and could feel the anger rising in my chest.

"I tried, Mary Beth. I tried to stay, and I just can't do it anymore. Do you see?"

I could see. I saw it in the sadness that hung in your eyes. I had seen it all year as I watched you unravel. I knew this was what you needed, and the reality of it all hit me. "I'm going to miss you," I whispered.

You let out a sad laugh and put a gentle hand on my arm. "I doubt that. You have your own adventure ahead of you."

"I guess that's true," I said. I suddenly felt very foolish. "I'm sorry. I don't know why I am acting like this. I don't really have a right to be upset over the choices you make for your life."

"It's okay. You have a right to be curious and even to be upset. We can talk about it, if it helps."

I nodded. I did have questions. "Why Portland?"

You shrugged. "It's beautiful. You know how I went there for a vacation a few years ago now? I can't explain it, it just felt like it could be . . . good for me."

"Will you ever come back?"

"I don't know," you answered honestly.

I sniffled and wiped a tear from my cheek. "Will we stay in touch?"

"I think we can." You nodded. You reached for my hand and gave it a small squeeze, in reassurance. You glanced over your shoulder and turned back to me, your eyes filled with kindness and something I couldn't name. "I should get back."

"Wait," I said, as you walked away. I fished in my purse for the letter I had written to you. I pulled it out and extended it to you. "I wrote this for you. It was a project for graduation. I didn't have time to get it to you at the ceremony," I said.

You smiled, took my letter, and walked back to the patio. Everyone asked you questions about your new adventure, and you showed off pictures of your future home. I watched and listened in a cloud of sadness. The barbeque ended with the setting sun, and we all left in a series of well wishes. I dropped Maverick off at his house and drove home.

A few weeks later, my parents attended a going-away party thrown in your honor, one that had been for adults only. And then you were gone, off to start a new life in Portland.

I didn't realize then how abnormal my reaction had been. I remember watching my peers react to your news and thinking, *Why aren't they more upset about this?* I thought this move you were making was a sort of cry for help, but there was nothing I could do to answer. I knew that this next stage of our relationship was gray and fragile. I was sure it wouldn't withstand the distance. How could it when the boundaries were so unclear? What did an appropriate relationship look like between a girl and her former teacher? Could we talk? Would we text? Would I ever have an excuse to see you again without crossing a line drawn in the sand?

With the gift of time (and therapy), I have learned that the reason our relationship persisted after high school was actually because it was never appropriate in the first place. I can see now that my emotional response can be explained by the way that you had allowed me to occupy a space in your life that should never have been mine. It has become clear to me that the real reason our relationship withstood the distance was because you continued to use me. Because of the power dynamic that existed between us as teacher and student, I continued to make myself available for you. And the consequence of all of this was that I was there. I was always just there. In many ways, I still am.

28

An Artifact

> *"I thought it would be nice to send you an old-fashioned card complete with real handwriting (okay, printing but beggars can't be choosers)."*

Mr. Davis,

I've struggled for a long time with how to start this letter. I suppose I should just begin by saying thank you, for everything. These past four years would have been nearly impossible if I did not have you to teach and to mentor me. I hope that you never feel like your efforts to help us students go unnoticed. I can honestly say that we treasure your advice, and are filled with gratitude for the time and effort you give to ensure our success. You once said that you almost left to teach somewhere else, and I want to thank you for not leaving us. I know with complete certainty that I would not be where I am today if you had.

Freshman year I knew that I loved to sing, but I did not have the confidence to share that. That is until you gave me voice lessons. You gave me the confidence to sing in front of others, and soon enough I could sing in front of the entire audience in *Seussical*. Thank you for encouraging me to take private voice lessons, sending me to the Regional Choral Showcase, pushing me to audition for the regional honor choir (which I would not have done either year if not for you), and for always being willing to help me improve my vocal skills. Thank you for coming to the honor choir to sit with me at lunch because I knew no one there. Thank you for spending countless hours making musical tracks for us. Thank you for all that you have done to prepare me for college, both musically and mentally.

Furthermore, you have inspired me as a person. Thank you for always giving me the right advice, and for helping me to get through these past four years. You have helped me to stand up for myself, which was very scary at first. Now, I still hesitate, but I feel more confident that it is the right thing to do. Even though I've made many mistakes, like Aaron ;), I have never felt that you were against me. Thank you for that.

You never need to apologize to me for the show choir not getting off to a great start this year. If I am being honest, I only joined because I felt that I wanted to be a part of helping you to start something new. Thank you for everything you did for us this year. I understand that it was difficult, and I can't thank you enough for all you did.

I never told you, but a few months ago I was asked to write an essay for college to explain why I chose to become a teacher. Immediately I knew the answer, and the essay was quite simple. In short my answer was, "I want to be a student's Mr. Davis. I want to be a positive role model for students who need one. I want to inspire, advise, and help students the way Mr. Davis has for me." Not one word of my essay was a lie. This summer, when I was considering my future career path, I decided that I want to teach because I want to be that person a student can look up to the way I look up to you.

You told me once that I am like you were in high school. I hope you're right. If I can become the kind of teacher that you are, I will reach my goal. I know I keep reiterating this, but I cannot stress enough what you've done for me. I may have disliked school for the people I had to deal with, but I am incredibly sad to leave because I will miss your direction. Choir class was not always the best, but it was always my favorite part of the day because I got to have you as a teacher.

I am terrified to leave high school, and the comfort of what I know; however, I am prepared and excited. As I leave, I will carry with me all that you have taught me. I will audition for collegiate choirs, and will attempt to find a voice teacher. I may have shied away from teaching music because of the lack of jobs, but I will never be without it in my life.

Your Student,

Mary Beth Wilson

29

Reunion

"You have become a very special person to me and I am so glad for you reentering my life."

College—Year One

In December 2013, it had been five months since I had seen you, and I was experiencing a type of withdrawal. When someone is woven into the fibers of your life so intrinsically, it is difficult to untangle the connection. Every now and then, in order to manage the symptoms of life without you, I would send you a text. Usually, the message would include an update on my journey to find a musical outlet in college and a question about your life in Portland. We would message back and forth for a couple of hours, and then eventually you would end the conversation with well wishes and a prompt to be sure to message with any updates in the future. It was during one of these exchanges that you told me you would be coming back home for Christmas.

I was thrilled that you would be home and immediately started scheming. I could not stand the thought of missing a chance to see you, especially when I was not guaranteed another opportunity. At the time, I was positive that you would draw the line at meeting with a former female student alone. Now, I know better.

I began recruiting my friends. I texted Maverick first and practically begged him to say yes. Once he was officially in, I reached out to our high school a cappella group to see who would be in the area around Christmas. I even included a few of the current students who I thought would jump at the chance to see you. After all, I was not the only one who idolized you. I had not spoken to many of them since graduation, which admittedly made this a bit of an awkward invite. I told myself it was worth it though, for a chance to spend an hour or two with you.

I made all of the plans. I organized the group, picked a spot for lunch, and set the date. I sent you the details in a casual invite, implying that we had already planned to meet, with or without you. I prayed you would agree to join us, and to my delight, you did so willingly.

The day of our mini reunion, Maverick and I pulled into the Olive Garden parking lot. I tugged at my sweater and made quick work of applying my lip gloss as Maverick scanned the parking lot for you. "He's by the door!" Maverick exclaimed as he turned to open the car door. "We must be the first ones. I don't see anyone else."

I took a deep breath, grabbed my purse, and followed.

"Davis! How the hell are ya?" yelled Maverick, who was already scurrying across the lot. I giggled but kept my pace, not wanting to appear overeager.

I stepped up onto the sidewalk with a timid smile. You were dressed almost entirely in denim, with dark jeans and a light, sherpa-lined jacket. Your hair was set perfectly, as it always was, and you held your brown leather bag in place with a hand across your chest. I thought you were beautiful there, in the cold December sunlight.

"There she is." You smiled and I was filled with warmth, despite the chill in the air.

"Here I am," I returned, relaxing into the familiarity of our rapport.

"It's good to see you, kid." You stepped to my side, placing your arm around my shoulder and pulling me into what my peers would joke was a "side hug." I returned the embrace, with a hand around your side, pretending I too found this to be a casual gesture. Meanwhile, I had to remind myself to breathe through the electricity that was suddenly running through my veins.

"Don't look now, but Deliah and Lacy are here . . . " Maverick whispered, disgust across his features.

I laughed and took a step away from you, worried that my approaching peers would misinterpret our embrace. "Be nice," I warned Maverick, squeezing his hand.

You offered them greetings and received a hug from Lacy, who looked as excited as I felt. As you were catching up, I caught a glimpse of Macy, Megan, and Katie pulling into a spot nearby and waved with excitement. I felt giddy to have the group back together.

We made our way inside and waited as the hostess worked to pull together enough tables to accommodate our group. I kept in step with you, hoping to ensure adjacent spots at the table. We all slid into our seats and immediately began catching up with each other's adventures.

Macy and Megan were still in high school and regaled us with stories of your "inferior" replacement. Lacy was attending a local university and had been upset by the lack of a campus a cappella group. Deliah was working at Starbucks and utilizing the community college to knock out her general education classes. Maverick filled us in on the lackluster dating pool at his university and had us all in tears as we laughed at his horror stories. Katie was the only other student who had moved away, like me. She was in Tennessee and found the extra warmth and general hospitality of the Southern state to be superior to our Midwestern town.

As the waitress came to collect our plates, I was filled with dread. The idea that our time together was ending so soon made me tense. When she returned to ask about the checks, Lacy was quick to announce that we would be paying separately. Our waitress nodded and said, "Okay, so everyone separate?"

"Oh, actually," I raised my hand, preparing to let her know that I would be paying for Maverick's meal because he had forgotten his debit card at home.

"Oh sure, you two are together?"

The moment hung in the air awkwardly as I realized she was gesturing toward you.

My cheeks felt like they were on fire. I tried to laugh casually, but it came out as a squeak instead. "Oh my God, no no. No, this one here." I fumbled to indicate that Maverick was my partner.

"Oh, sorry," she said, looking uncertain as to why I was acting so foolish.

She turned to walk away. Deliah let out an exaggerated laugh, which sent the table into a fit of hysterics. I hid my face in my hands, wishing I could evaporate before I had to face your response. Surely, you were appalled. I thought you might be angry at me for somehow making our waitress think we could be a couple.

"Why would she even say that? You're obviously twice her age," Deliah proclaimed, between laughs.

You shrugged. "It's not that weird. People with age gaps date all the time."

I pulled my face from my hands and turned to you, shocked by your response. You were seemingly unfazed by the chaos, sitting back in your chair with your legs crossed.

"Okay, but like fifteen years?" Lacy asked, looking between us as if trying to assess whether we looked like a suitable couple.

You ignored the others and looked at me earnestly. "Of course. I know a lot of happy couples with similar gaps. Mr. Fraser's wife is ten years younger than him, and they're very happy."

I looked away quickly, hoping you wouldn't catch the hope filling my eyes. The logical part of me knew you were saying these things in an attempt to diffuse an awkward situation. I was nearly certain these words were not meant to be about you and me specifically. Even so, my heart swelled at the idea that maybe you were intentionally speaking to downplay the barrier that stood between us. I thought about that night at my house when you declared it would not be so strange if you were to flirt with me if you hadn't been my teacher.

"Yeah, well, you were her teacher, and it's weird." Deliah shrugged and pushed her chair. "Anyway, I can't stay. I have to get to work. Let us know next time you're home, Davis." She shrugged into her coat and turned to go without acknowledging the rest of us.

Within the next few minutes, our checks were paid, and we had no reason to stay. Slowly, we all started to stand, pushing our chairs in and slipping our arms into our coats.

Katie spoke first. "I know we should leave, but I don't want to go sit at my house with my parents. Anyone want to walk over to Starbucks with me and grab a coffee?"

With the exception of Lacy, the rest of our crew agreed as we started to make our way to the parking lot. "What about you, Davis?" Maverick pressed. "Come on, you won't get to see this shining face for a long time."

To my surprise, you agreed to join us and we all walked across the parking lot together. Our party claimed every available seat in the small coffee shop with our coats draped over chairs. We all ordered our approximations of coffee and made our way back to our seats. I laughed at the contrast of your dark roast among our chai lattes and mocha Frappuccinos. Though we were on the cusp of adulthood, we had not yet acquired a taste for coffee.

I slid into my seat with my latte as you stayed behind to stir some cream into your coffee. Macy motioned for me to lean in close and whispered, "Oh my God, MB. He misses you."

"Shut up, he does not!" I hissed. I felt myself blush deeply and put a hand to my face, worried you might catch on to our conversation.

Macy and Megan giggled at my flustered reaction as you approached the table.

"What's so funny?" you asked, sliding into the seat next to me.

"They're just being dorks." I gave Macy a pointed look and took a quick sip of my drink, consequently burning my tongue.

You smiled as if you saw right through me but graciously changed the subject. "You know, I love coffee shops, but nothing beats the coffee I make at home."

"Oh yeah?" I took the lid off my cup, hoping it would start to cool a bit faster.

"Oh yes, I make a pour-over every morning. It takes a long time, but I don't mind. Actually, it forces me to slow down. Otherwise, mornings are wasted on tasks, and next thing I know I'm at work. Watching my coffee steep slowly through the filter makes me stop for a moment. I allow myself to sit down and drink it at home too. It's become a sort of morning ritual."

"I like that. I'm still trying to find some routine in my schedule, which feels silly because it is going to change again next semester. That's hard for me, you know? The constant change."

You nodded and looked away. You took a slow sip of your coffee, thinking over my words. Finally, you turned back, your kind eyes meeting mine. "Well, let's figure it out together. Find something that you enjoy that remains the same. We can start with that."

I considered your prompt, aware that my peers had slowly broken away from our conversation. "I've started running," I confessed. "It's actually been really nice. I listen to music and explore a bit of campus. It was really beautiful in the fall."

You peered at me over your coffee, your eyes full of skepticism. "You what now? If I remember correctly, last we spoke you were disgusted by your roommate's gross running habit."

You did remember that night. Did you remember the other things that were said? I shoved the thought down as fast as I could and rolled my eyes at your dramatics. "Yeah well, it grew on me. Nikki wakes up and goes to the gym or for a run early every morning. At first it was annoying how disciplined she was, getting up at the first ring of her alarm and everything. Then, one day she invited me to go and I did, reluctantly. After that, I started joining when I could. Next thing I knew I was going by myself willingly."

"Well look at you, a real athlete." The sarcasm was dripping from your voice, and we both laughed at the idea of anyone mistaking me for an athlete. "You don't get up with your first alarm?"

"Oh absolutely not . . . that seems impossible. Do you?"

"How else would I have time for my coffee ritual?" you asked, raising an eyebrow. "Admittedly, I take a long time to get dressed and ready for the day; I need every minute I can get."

I put my hand to my mouth and tried to keep from giggling at you. "Well, there's a workaround for that," I claimed through laughter. "I have no less than five alarms starting at least thirty minutes before I have to get up."

This time you laughed. "There's always one. In every pair there's one who gets up right away and one who drives them crazy snoozing the alarm."

"Alright, you two, let us in on the joke!" Maverick sneered as he shoved his way between us, popping the bubble I hadn't realized surrounded us.

"Oh my God, MB! You have to tell everyone about that boy who is teaching you how to play guitar. It's sooooooo romantic," Maverick cooed, pressing his head to my shoulder theatrically.

Macy and Megan perked up, immediately demanding the details. You looked at me, eyes full of curiosity.

"It's not really working out. I can't get my fingers to press the strings down enough!" I exclaimed, hoping to change the conversation to focus on my own lack of skill rather than the college boy in question.

"I didn't know you wanted to learn," you said earnestly. "You should have said something. I could help you."

"I didn't really," I shrugged and took a sip of my now-cooled latte. "He offered . . . "

"And he's super cute!" Maverick crowed, cutting me off and causing my palms to sweat with embarrassment.

"Well, in that case . . . " You gave me a look that made me wish I could evaporate. "But really, getting the strings down just takes strength, practice, and calluses. If you want to learn, just stick with it."

I shrugged. "I'll try, I guess. We've been practicing all semester. I prefer piano . . . well, actually, I prefer to sing while someone else plays for me."

"Fair enough. Sounds like you have someone for that anyway." You winked at me, and I buried my face in my latte.

From the other side of the table, Katie spoke up, saving me. "At least you have a shot at doing music, MB. I cannot find anyone interested in performing at school. It sucks."

We spent hours like that, chatting as the winter sun dissolved into the clouds. Unfortunately, we could not delay the inevitable. Megan, Macy, and Katie left first with quick goodbyes. Maverick and I stayed behind, attempting to clean up the space and put the chairs we had moved back in their original placements. You helped and walked to the parking lot with us.

"Well, you two, this was really nice," you said sincerely. You turned to me, placing a gentle hand on my shoulder. "Thank you for everything. I know you were the mastermind here, and I am grateful to you, as always."

I always felt proud when you acknowledged me, but something about the way you were looking at me made my pulse race in a new way. I looked down, avoiding the heat of your gaze. "I'm just glad we could see you. We've missed you."

"Well, I am freezing my tits off. It's been real. See ya, Davis!" Maverick sang, as he sprinted to the car.

I lingered, unsure how to make my feet move away from you. I think you sensed my hesitancy because you stayed behind, too.

"Hey," you said, your voice low, "we'll talk soon."

"I know," I said, meeting your eyes. My sadness hung there in the air between us until I felt tears burning my eyes. I tried to wipe them away quickly, knowing how silly I must look to you. Even so, I felt myself speaking before I could stop. "Will I ever see you again?"

You laughed. "Well, would you like to?"

I rolled my eyes at that. "Of course I would."

"Then, I would say so, yes." You gave me a playful nudge. "Now go. We'll talk."

Reluctantly, I started to move away. "Goodbye, forever."

"Goodbye, forever," you mocked, with a smile.

When I got into the car, Maverick was gawking at me, his eyes full of mischief. "Shut up!" I said before he could say a word.

That night, I received a string of pictures from Macy captioned "love birds." In each one, you and I were seated at that big table, laughing at each other. I noticed the way your legs were turned in toward me, and my arm rested on the table, inches from yours. I kept those photos for a long time, holding them as evidence that I hadn't imagined it all.

Graciously, you have given me proof since that it wasn't all in my imagination. That next December, you would affirm every look, every taunt, and every word that I clung to over our relationship. Whether or not you would claim them as such, these little moments were the tiny beginnings of the feelings you would soon make known.

30
Loss

"I think of you daily."

I am back in the auditorium. My theater director is standing up front, beaming with an announcement. He is announcing our senior musical. I am twenty-eight years old, but for some reason, this does not feel odd to me. I am with my fellow theater kids, all grown into the adult versions of ourselves. He announces the show and barely finishes before we break into excited squeals. We start gushing, sharing our dream roles for Into the Woods. I have been dreaming of playing a princess all my life, but not in this show. In this show I had my sights on the baker's wife. You knew this because we had talked about it once upon a time, a time that feels very far away at this moment. You start calling everyone over. One by one you run their range. You have them sing a sample of my dream role and it is like a stab to my heart—a stab that becomes fatal when I realize you have no intention of including me. I decide I will prepare for auditions and I will make you choose me. You will have to if I blow you away with my talent. I work until I am sure my performance is Tony-worthy. I show up the day of auditions to find you are cold and unwelcoming. Instead of showing you my skills, I leave in tears. I don't think I am sad about the role I may lose. Instead, I am devastated by the loss of my mentor and friend.

I wake and spend the rest of the night tossing in sleeplessness, haunted by the feeling that you might hate me forever.

31
Different

"I knew then that things were different between us and I had a lot to think about."

College—Year Two

It was the week of exams, and the first snow of the season had fallen. I sat at my little desk, staring at my psychology book. However, instead of focusing on studying, I found myself lost in thoughts of you. That night, I had a dream that I was back in your class, sitting next to you on the piano bench. In my sleep, you covered me in your sadness, and I held you close. I awoke, enveloped in that feeling and longing to know if you were okay. Unable to shake it, I decided a cup of coffee and a change in scenery might help clear the lingering haze. I pulled my blanket from my bed, shoved my books into my backpack, and made myself a cup of coffee. I padded down the quiet hall, coffee in hand, and searched for a study room.

I sat on the little couch, wrapped in my blanket. My book was open on my lap, but I stared at the snow-covered trees and sipped my coffee. I thought about you and your life in Portland. I wondered if you had found companionship and prayed you were happy there. I think you may never understand how deeply I cared for you, but that was the consequence of unloading your burdens on a child. Your existence was like a tide, always returning in waves that covered my feet when I dared to venture too far from shore. I debated whether it would help to check in with you and decided there was little harm in a quick message.

I pulled my phone out and typed a short text letting you know I had started singing with my campus church on Sunday mornings and missed our times leading worship together. I pressed send and returned my gaze to the window. I felt immediately lighter, knowing you would at least know I was thinking of you. I didn't have to wait long; within minutes, you responded. You congratulated me on my newest endeavor and shared that you had found a church yourself. Then, you shared that you reclaimed your life as a follower of Christ. According to my circle at the time, this was one of the single most pivotal moments of an individual's life. I was thrilled for you. I shared my joy and pressed, asking for more details about this new journey. Instead of answering, you suggested it was a story better shared in person and asked if I would be interested in grabbing coffee while I was home for Christmas break.

I did try to keep our unspoken boundaries; I promise I did. I messaged my group of friends and asked if anyone would be interested in joining us, like they had last year. However, I had decided to work that week, so my availability was slim. The morning of our scheduled meetup, I reluctantly texted you to let you know that the only other person to agree to join (Maverick) had canceled on us at the last minute. I was so sure you would think better of meeting with a teenage girl alone, but you didn't. Instead, you responded, "No worries, I'll see you at 4."

I had worked at the daycare that day and was disheveled after a long day. I punched out promptly at 3:30 p.m. and rushed to the bathroom to freshen up. There was absolutely no way I would be meeting you in such a state. I was currently dressed in jeans and a T-shirt, with my makeup having melted away by a day spent chasing toddlers. The moment I clocked out, I grabbed the bag I had packed and tucked myself away in the staff bathroom to change. I locked myself in a cramped stall. I shed my work clothes and struggled to stay upright as I wriggled my tights up over my thighs. With effort, I managed to change into my cream-colored sweater dress and matching tall socks. I pulled on my boots, zipped them up to my knees, and haphazardly shoved my work clothes into my bag. Once I had made all of the adjustments needed to my outfit, I touched up my blush, powdered the shine away from my face, and brushed mascara over my lashes. I pulled my fallen curls into a loose ponytail and secured it with a silky green bow. I took one last look in the mirror. Foolishly, I found myself hoping you might notice the way my face had lost some of its youth. I had grown my bangs out and dyed my hair back to its natural, deeper brown. It's not that I thought you would be attracted to me, which felt unlikely and inappropriate. I just wished for your approval and aspired to look as grown as I felt.

I drove down the street and pulled into the coffee shop parking lot with a racing heart. Something about meeting with you like this felt unusual. We had been alone together and had plenty of experience carrying conversations without the help of others. Why, then, was I so nervous? I shut off the engine and turned toward the entrance, wondering if I had been first to arrive. As I walked across the parking lot, I contemplated whether I should order my drink or wait for you. I wondered if I should lay claim to the comfortable chairs by the windows or get a more formal seat at a table. Thankfully, you stopped this train of thought, walking up behind me as I reached for the door.

"There she is." I turned and saw you were smiling at me just a few steps back, your eyes squinting in the winter sunlight. You were dressed in jeans and a soft gray cardigan. The sunlight brought out the freckles over your cheeks and danced in the deep locks of your hair, which had been cut shorter. I remember thinking that you were as handsome as I remembered and immediately wishing I hadn't noticed, as a new wave of nervous adrenaline rushed through my body.

"Hey." I smiled, stopping with my hand on the door.

The smell of roasted coffee and synthetic pine invaded my senses as you stepped forward and took the door from my hand. For a brief moment, we stood so close I could feel your chest against my shoulder. With a deep breath, I forced myself to take a step to the side and allowed you to open the door.

We entered the shop and approached the counter together. I paused, unsure if I should cut in front of you or wait behind. Graciously, you stepped back and gestured for me to order first. I nodded in thanks and placed my order for a café au lait, which had become my go-to coffee order on campus.

You smirked and took a step closer, placing yourself next to me at the counter. "Since when do you drink real coffee?"

"Since I needed it to keep up with eighteen credit hours of schoolwork and projects." I blushed as I pulled out my debit card.

You placed a hand on mine, stopping me in my tracks. "This one's on me."

I gave you a look of skepticism, testing your sincerity. It wasn't that I worried you couldn't afford my two dollar coffee order. This gesture felt intimate, especially with the way your hand brushed against mine. I tried to gather the words to speak, to ask if you were okay with the implications of paying for my drink, but you didn't give me the time. You pulled your hand from mine, told the barista to make a second, and slid your card into the machine without pause.

"Thanks," I said softly, attempting to maintain composure.

You seemed unfazed as you walked past me, scanning the room for a pair of seats. "So, tell me about college."

"Oh, you know, it's good. I'm just busy." I followed you as I spoke. To my delight, you selected the cozy nook near the windows and placed your shoulder bag on the floor next to one of the brown leather chairs. I shrugged out of my winter coat and laid it across the back of the other chair with my purse.

The barista called out our order, and I spun to head back to the counter. You put your hand to my arm, stopping me. "I'll get it, you sit."

The leather of the seat was heated from the sun and I soaked in the rare December warmth as I waited for your return. Despite my efforts to remain calm, I found myself wondering what was going through your head. I wondered if you felt obligated to come or whether you wished you could have bailed with the others. With each second my confidence dwindled, and I started to feel like a very silly girl who was obsessed with her teacher.

Thankfully, you sank into your seat moments later and handed my coffee to me across the table, mercifully interrupting my thoughts. I felt myself relax when I saw you smiling at me, as if you knew to disprove my insecurities. We sipped our coffees in silence for a moment before you spoke.

"So, you're going to be a teacher?" you asked, even though you had known my major since I enrolled.

"Yup, that's the plan. Sometimes I feel unsure about it, though. It just seems like the system is such a mess. Every time I am in class, they talk about this career like it's the greatest thing you'll ever do." I threw my hands up to emphasize my point. "But it feels like they are just overselling it, you know? I mean, it's a job, not a lifestyle. Why do we have to be so heroic about it?"

"That's a keen observation," you said, sitting up a bit. "You are wise beyond your years, Mary Beth Wilson."

I put my coffee to my lips, hoping to hide my face as pride swelled in my chest at the compliment. I only ever wanted to be as wise as you.

"How about you?" I asked, diverting the focus from myself. "Are you enjoying teaching up there in Portland?"

"You know, it's just a job." A slow smile spread across your face, and I giggled as you continued. "I mean, the job is fine. The kids are great." You wrapped your hands around your coffee cup and turned toward me in your seat. "Portland is beautiful. The hiking is breathtaking, and I've been enjoying that more as I find the time. It is a bit lonely sometimes. I haven't lived as a bachelor in a very long time, and I am still learning what that looks like for me. I use school a lot to fill my time, but it's not the same as it was before. I don't have the community and the kids don't know me yet, so the work is mostly building rapport and trust with them. You'll learn this when you start your career, but that trust you build with your students is more important than anything they're teaching you in your courses." (You were right. I do know this now.)

I smiled. Seeing your humanity outside of school was always refreshing. It was a welcome shift in the dynamic as we settled into our new roles. I spoke slowly, attempting to select words that would highlight my maturity. "I'm sure. Obviously, I don't know much about what it's like to be married, but I imagine it is a completely different way of living. I mean, having a roommate has already changed the way I live." I mentally cringed at my attempt to compare my college experience with your adult reality. "I think you should give yourself grace. It doesn't have to come easily, and you don't have to be alone through it. You are rediscovering a life; I mean, that's why you moved to Portland, right? To have a fresh start and to do that in peace? Your students will love you, and I am sure they already trust you. I always did. I still do."

You sat back and looked at me for a long moment. I struggled to hold your gaze, melting a bit under the intensity. Something about the way you were looking at me felt different. It felt like you were looking at me for the first time, analyzing me as if we hadn't met before this moment.

"What?" I asked, surrendering under the pressure and sweeping my eyes to the floor.

"You." You leaned closer and propped your head on your arm against the chair. "You're just so grown up. It took me many years and a lot of mistakes to learn the things you already seem to understand." You shook your head in disbelief. "How old are you now?"

"I turned nineteen in September," I said. "But I feel older. I always have. I think that's why I have trouble making friends my age. Don't even get me started about dating." I rolled my eyes and fiddled with the lid of my cup.

"Well, you should give yourself grace too, I think." You smiled, and leaned back into your chair. "I am confident you will find your people. You have always been ahead of your time. College boys aren't ready for you. Give them a chance to grow up a bit."

I laughed at that and set my coffee on the side table. "Maybe that's my problem. College boys are the worst, you know. A guy I went on a date with recently told me that he wouldn't make it official with me until I was able to show him I had 'accessed the Holy Spirit' by speaking tongues." I put up air quotes for emphasis and scoffed.

"That's absurd," you said, through laughter. "Did you speak in tongues for him?"

"Of course not!" I exclaimed, giving you a playful nudge on the shoulder before I thought better of touching you. Thankfully, you did not rebuke me, but laughed harder in return.

We sat there laughing and chatting together for hours. I noticed that the formality between us was melting away into something that felt unexpectedly comfortable.

Our cups sat on the table, empty, as the orange glow of the setting sun spilled over us. I was laughing at something you said about your new students' absolute inability to sight read, which sparked a question I had been meaning to ask. "Oh, I have been wanting to ask you this. Did you know I am actually not an alto? I auditioned for the Women's Chorus at school and she placed me as a soprano one. I went from the lowest voice to the highest?!"

"Of course I knew that," you said. "Your upper register was stronger than any other high schooler in the choir. Remember when I gave you the top part in a cappella because it was too high for Deliah to do well? Problem is, you could harmonize and they couldn't. I put you where you were needed."

My jaw dropped. "Excuse me? You knew?" I was a little bit angry at this revelation. I had spent years thinking I was an alto. I thought my upper register was my weakness, but I also struggled to believe my lower register was a strength. I ended up feeling like I just didn't quite fit anywhere. "You could have at least told me."

You put your hands up defensively, "Hey, I did it for you too. Anyway, you had the range. Learning to harmonize is what made you a well-rounded singer. Plus, did you really want to stand with the sopranos every day? I'm so sorry to have kept you from that joy." You laughed, put your hands on your knees, and stood. "Anyway, I'm thirsty. You want some water?" You asked as you leaned over me to grab our empty cups.

"Sure," I said. I became suddenly aware of the way my dress was riding up my thighs in my seat and tugged at the edges.

You walked away, and I sat once again alone with my thoughts. Something about you was softer. It wasn't that I hadn't experienced your vulnerability before—I recalled those nights at rehearsals when you confided in me. This was different though. You were speaking to me as a friend. I dared to believe that you were almost being flirtatious with me.

You came back and handed me a cup filled with water. You sat in your seat and took a sip of your water, your eyes on me. Then, you leaned back casually. "So, you want to hear my 'Prodigal Son' story?"

"I really do," I returned, sitting up to show you I was interested.

You launched into the story of your path to a little church in town. You told me about the sadness that had consumed you and the brokenness that left you feeling unworthy of companionship. My heart ached for you. Mercifully, a coworker introduced you to his friend, who happened to be a pastor. This pastor brought you into his church, hoping you could revitalize a dying worship team. What started as a project to distract you from your loneliness brought you into a community that accepted you as you were. Eventually, this led you to choosing to follow Jesus and adapting your lifestyle to fit the one that you believed He had planned for you.

When you finished, I was overwhelmed. "I am so glad for you, Mr. Davis. I have always prayed that you would find peace."

"Me too," you said softly, leaning closer to me.

"I hope you know, you don't have to be lonely." I offered, hoping you would catch my meaning. I never wanted you to feel alone. I was here and had vowed to myself I would stay as long as you needed me. I hoped you knew that you always had me here. I was simply waiting for you to ask.

"I know that." You smiled, leaning in to place a hand on the edge of my chair and glancing out the window. The darkness was settling around us, and I could feel the night closing in and threatening our time together. "I hate to say this, but I have to go soon," you said quietly, not moving away.

My heart sank as I realized this was the end. I considered the reality that this may be the last time I saw you for another year and swallowed against the rising lump in my throat. I nodded and started to move to grab my purse. You reached for my arm and held me there. I turned back and we sat like that for a beat, neither of us wanting to break the spell of this time together, whatever it meant.

"Walk out with me? Please. I want to give you something," you said.

I nodded. "Okay."

We walked out together and you placed a hand on my back, guiding me in the direction of your car. You opened the trunk and dug around in the pile of bins before pulling out a thin, red book. "Here," you said, holding it out to me. "I loved this book. I think you will too. I will read it again with you, if you'd like. Maybe we could talk about it together?"

I took the book and nodded. "I would like that."

I slid the book into my bag and looked back at you. I felt awkward, unsure how to start a goodbye. As I considered my options, you stepped forward and pulled me into your arms. Hesitantly, I returned your embrace and you stepped in closer, dipping your head against mine. We stood there for what was likely a few seconds but felt like an eternity. I could feel you breathing and wished there was a way to bottle up a moment. I wanted to preserve this feeling for a lifetime. Finally, you stepped back and smiled. "I'll see you soon, MB."

"Promise?" I asked.

"I promise," you returned, tucking an escaped curl back in place behind my ear.

I walked to my car and drove home in silence. Even my mind was not sure where to start. It was as if it was frozen in time. By the time I pulled into my driveway, I was starting to thaw back into reality. I started to wonder if I had imagined it, or if what was left of the line between us had faded with the sun as we sat there together. Luckily, no one was waiting for me in the kitchen, and I was able to hide away in my room. I pulled out the book you had given me. I looked at the title, *Crazy Love*. I had heard of this book from my

Christian peers. It was well renowned and had been suggested to me before. I opened it and started reading.

I couldn't focus though, My mind was swirling with the memories from the evening. I set the book aside and surrendered to the tornado of feelings in my head. I thought of the way you called me "wise," the playfulness about my dating life, the feeling of your arms around me. I couldn't make sense of it all within the context of our relationship. This felt distinctly different. This felt like friendship. This felt like more than that. I had been on a few dates and found myself comparing our time together with what I recognized from those experiences. I laid out the facts for analysis. We were alone. You paid for my drink. You had been kind and thoughtful and sought to know me better. You made me feel special and treated me with kindness. You had lacked the formality of a teacher and his student and crossed the lines between us with very little hesitation. This wasn't a date. I knew it wasn't a date. Though I couldn't deny that on paper, this really did seem like it may have been.

I needed to distract myself before I spiraled into dangerous territory. I reached for my phone, pressed my passcode in, and swiped to unlock the screen. Before I could open my social media app, I saw a new text from you.

```
Let me know what you think of the book. I'll start
rereading. It was good to see you. Thanks for
listening.
```

I started to type a response but stopped as three little dots appeared, indicating you were still typing.

```
PS: I think you can start calling me William. ;)
```

32
Love

"In Christ's (and my own) Love."

College—Year Two

My sophomore year of college, I lived with a girl named Kristy, who was a fellow education major and honors college student. When Nikki had decided to become a resident advisor in our sophomore year, leaving me without a room-mate, Kristy came to my rescue. Living with Kristy was the safest I ever felt in those four years. In an interview about his collaboration with Emma Stone, Andrew Garfield once said, "She was like a shot of espresso. She's like being bathed in the sunlight." Add a sentence about her being a compassionate, fierce friend, and this is Kristy.

Every now and then, when our schedules aligned, Kristy and I would sneak away to the music building on campus. We would climb the stairs to the third floor in hopes that a practice room was open. Each practice room was small, about the perfect size for two to fit comfortably, but certainly no more. There was a piano, a bench, and a small chair set in the corner. Here, tucked away from the world in a partially soundproof room, I would play the piano and sing while Kristy lay on the floor, staring comfortably at the ceiling.

One afternoon, Kristy and I had been in the piano room for what may have been ten minutes, but was quite possibly an hour.

I had spent my time learning to play "Make You Feel My Love" by Adele. When I had my first, solid run-through of the song, Kristy popped up from her spot on the floor. "Who are you singing about?" The question hung in the air as she climbed onto the piano bench. I think she noticed the hesitation in my silence. She wrapped her arm around mine in encouragement and leaned her head on my shoulder before she continued to press. "Who do you love, MB?"

The question danced in my mind, twirling through the thoughts of you. I had not told anyone about us yet, not even my closest friends. I hadn't been ready to invite anyone else into our bubble in case their judgments might prick at its delicate surface. However, the pressure of keeping the growing secret was threatening enough that I decided it was time to share with someone.

I grabbed Kristy's arm and lay my head against hers on my shoulder. "There is something I haven't told you," I sighed. "It's my choir director."

Kristy gasped and pulled her face away so that she was looking into my eyes. "Oh my God. Tell me everything."

She grabbed my hand and looked genuinely interested in my story. There was so much assurance in her eyes that I launched into the entire tale. I told her about high school and every kindness you offered to me. I shared about the ways you made me feel like I was your favorite and the time you called me beautiful. I told her about the brokenness I witnessed and how badly I wanted to hold you together. I shared the story of our coffee date and how our relationship had progressed ever since.

When I finished, she took my face in her hands and said, without a hint of judgment, "You love him." It wasn't a question.

"Yeah, I think I do. I think I have loved him for a long time," I confessed.

Kristy turned her body toward mine and tucked her legs up onto the bench. "How does that make you feel?"

"I just, I am not sure how it happened. It's like there is no single thing about him that I love. There is nothing he could say or do that would make me stop. There is no 'I love him because.' There's just, 'I love him.'" I sighed. It was frustrating how incomplete this expression felt. There were not enough words to convey how I felt about you. Now, of course, I know why.

Kristy was thoughtful. She considered my words for a moment before pressing me to consider a new depth of emotion. She asked, "Are you in love with him? It's different. You love him, sure, but are you in love with him?"

I wasn't sure how to answer that question. I had very little experience with love. In my nineteen years of life, I had told two boys that I loved them. I had only meant it once. Even so, I knew I had never felt like this before. This feeling bordered on something more like obsession.

During this time, when I was nineteen, you had a lot to say to me about love. You sent me paragraphs about the lack of intimacy you felt with your wife. You told me that love was not a matter of falling—that was too "haphazard," according to your expertise. You told me that love was a matter of choice and was not to be taken lightly. You sent me articles about Christian love and verses that were to be used as models. Once, when I expressed that I cared deeply for you, you cautioned me to avoid the "L word." You told me that we offer "more than a kind word" when we say that we love someone and that we should not take that lightly.

You misunderstood. I knew exactly what I meant when I said I cared deeply for you. I meant that I loved you. I am not sure why you were shocked by this revelation. Maybe you just did not want to hear it from me because it would confirm just how wrong this was. You always acted as though that time at Starbucks was a "first meeting," as if the years I had spent as your student didn't count. You said you wanted to "get to know me," as if I had not shared every single intimate detail of my life with you for four years.

Well, I am grown now, and I am confident that I know about love. I know what it looks like and what it doesn't. To be frank, I think I may know more about love than you did when you wrote to me all those years ago.

I used to think love was a helpless emotion. I thought it was a feeling that came suddenly and there was nothing anyone could do about it. When I was fourteen, I fell in love with Aaron. What began as an immediate attraction to a tall, attractive boy with great hair and far more talent than his peers grew into a desire to know him and to be known by him. When Aaron was near, I could feel the heat of flickering embers radiating in my veins. Aaron did not simply make me feel seen. He was the first boy who really saw me. He noticed when I felt anxious and anticipated my desires. He took interest in the things that excited me and showed me parts of himself he kept reserved. If we were in a crowded room, Aaron would reach for me. He would pull me to him and hold me without any expectation that I would give him more. Aaron met me exactly where I was and never pushed me to give him what I was not ready to offer. He loved me in a way I didn't quite grasp at the time. I think he loved me beyond the feeling, into a realm of devotion that I had no reference for at the time. I know now that I was too immature for the type of love he offered. Instead, Aaron became my story of lost love. The kind that never settles, but floats. A love that becomes untethered but is never quite gone. A choice unmade, but a lingering respect for another.

When I met my husband, the falling in love was easy and notable. I was immediately attracted to his physical presence. He was a college football player, and I recall forcing shaky breaths as I watched him do workouts with his teammates on the beach that week we met. Then, I made him laugh for the first time. He had this giggle that would project his joy onto an entire room. I wanted to be the one to make him laugh forever. One night, I started to feel the familiar glow in my heart as he grabbed a guitar and sang for me under the twinkling lights, our feet dangling in the cool water. Weeks later, we sat in the student union, sipping smoothies together between classes. I told him I wanted to run back to my dorm and put on makeup before an event that evening. He stared at me with an awestruck expression. I asked him what he was thinking. There was a beat of silence, which I now know was the time it took for him to choose his words and assess whether they were worth sharing, which is one of my favorite things about him. After a moment, he responded simply, "You are just so . . . beautiful." My whole heart oozed at the confession. The more I learned about that tender man, the more I fell into love. He was incredibly sensitive, but stronger than any man I had known. He was the silliest guy in the room, but also, somehow the smartest. He never said anything he didn't mean, and he was never content with any information or circumstance until he fully understood. Falling in love with him was easy and natural. Within a month, we had confirmed it with words. We were in love.

I have loved so many people in my life, I couldn't possibly write it out. I love my family with a love so strong it could move mountains. My love for my friends is so loyal that I would commit unspeakable crimes for them. I love my children with a love so big it could push against the sky and reach into galaxies not yet discovered.

Love has taken many sizes, shapes, and forms. Love has come and gone. It has been lost and found. Love, it turns out, is not a simple feeling. It is a complex knot, tied together by choice, devotion, and emotion.

All this is to say, I think that I did love you, in a way. Every time I cried to you about my silly high school relationships and you took my side, I fell. When I felt insecure and you built me up with encouragement and praise, you took up space in my heart. When you let me support you, but insisted that only I could be trusted to do so, that space grew. I loved you when I was your student. This love I developed over that time was the kind of toxic love that would have followed you anywhere. I would have taken your side relentlessly. I believed you, and I believed in you. That's why when you told me that it was okay for us to pursue a relationship outside the boundaries of social norms, I believed you. When you said that the pressures from society and pushback we may have received from others was merely an obstacle for us to overcome together, I believed you.

But let's not forget, you told me love is a choice. I think that is true and it isn't. I fell in love with my husband, but I chose to nurture that love. I make choices every day to sustain the love that I have decided is important.

I never had a choice in the matter when it came to you. I never chose to love you. I was, quite simply, your apprentice. You had power over me, in both a metaphorical and very literal way. This is why relationships between two individuals are forbidden when one of those individuals holds power over the other. Bosses are not allowed to date their employees. Romantic relationships between professors and their students are prohibited. Even relationships between two individuals whose age gap spans between teenage to adult years are frowned upon. All this is because we recognize that love is not fair when it develops underneath the leadership of another. When one party yields the authority to dictate the shape it takes, the choice in the matter falls away. What was left was a girl who loved the man that watched her grow up. A girl who designed so much of the woman she was becoming around what her teacher had suggested to be the "right path" for her.

I looked up to you and you let me down. I had no choice before, and sometimes I wonder if I ever will. Sometimes, I feel stuck here in this love for you. I resist the urge to defend you every time someone says you are gross, or manipulative. I want to tell them that you "didn't mean it that way." You didn't groom me; you're just a really good teacher. I want to tell them that you loved me too, which is why you approached the shift in our relationship so gently. I have offered the suggestion that perhaps this was my fault. It was my fault that I loved you, and I somehow pushed you into this gray area. I have offered so many excuses for you so that I could keep loving you.

If love is a choice, know that I am actively choosing to stop loving you. It becomes a little easier, as I take my power back from you. Little by little, I reverse our dynamic. I now realize that I may be the only person who holds this secret, a secret that has the power to destroy reputations and relationships. With that power comes agency, and the more I lean into my ability to choose, the less I love you.

33
Thinking of You

"I hope this letter finds you well and in good spirits."

College—Year Two

Ten years ago, I retrieved my mail from the box in the lobby of my dorm. I padded upstairs, shifting through the stack. I noticed an envelope addressed with handwriting. This was a rarity. As a student, I didn't often receive personal mail. I opened the door to my room just as I read the name of the sender, William Davis.

I read your letter sitting on the twin bed in my dorm. I poured over every word until I reached the end. When I did, I read it again. I wondered how long it had taken you to decorate the cover as you did, with several lines drawn into the bark of a tree. In the center, there was a heart, drawn as if it had been scratched. Words were etched into the paper in several broken strokes. *Thinking of You.*

I have kept this letter for ten years, tucked away safely in an unsuspecting book. I have packed it away through several moves, always ensuring it found a space in my new home. When everything ended between us, it was like the rug had been pulled from beneath me. Every memory of you, tainted by new light. I wished I could throw it away. Maybe if I did, every piece of our relationship after graduation would disappear with it. Perhaps I could reclaim our story and remember you for the kind, exceptional teacher I once believed you to be.

I couldn't follow through. Every time I swore that I would finally rip your letter apart, I found myself tucking it back into safety on my bookshelf. The truth is that I knew that it wouldn't work, this attempt to clean our slate. So, instead of throwing the letter away, I started to share it. I was slow and particular about my choice to expose this piece of our story.

First, I shared it with my first boyfriend after you. Through tears I passed this letter to him as a confession. For the first time, I felt ashamed of you. *I had this relationship with my teacher.* I thought surely he would be angry with me—after all, this wasn't supposed to happen. Instead he said he was disgusted by you. He said it was unfair to me. He said he was so sorry. I didn't exactly get it, but I accepted his kindness. Our relationship progressed, and I married him a few short years later. He has remained my steadiest support, through the highs and lows of processing you.

Years later, I showed my therapist. She asked me to read your letter to her. I remember the pity on her face as she used phrases with words like "spiritual abuse," "grooming," and "inappropriate behavior." I didn't understand how someone could think those awful things about you. She helped me understand.

One night in 2022, I let my best friend, Hannah, read your letter. She was angry. She was angry at you. She helped me get the courage to cut our final ties, my last path to communicate with you. Together, we blocked your Facebook account. She said you should never be allowed to work in a school again. She said I was a child, and you were a man, a man who should've known better. She's sorry this happened to me. *Happened to me.* I thought that was such an interesting way to phrase it.

One winter day, I sat curled under my favorite blanket. I was snuggled up to Hannah, a cup of coffee wrapped in my hands. We had collected a couple of our favorite women and retreated to a cabin for quiet, slow days like this. The fireplace crackled and the snow danced through the air outside. Everything was picturesque, except for the feelings I couldn't shake. I had dreamed of you the night before, which had forced me to recall your time in my life. This is not an unusual occurrence. Unfortunately, it happens all the time. I hate it.

Like a creature of the night, my dreams often lose their power in the light. Instead of allowing the darkness to take hold, I chose to share my dream with the women. I told them about us and about the letter you wrote me, which had made its appearance in my dream.

I remember explaining it to them. "I just cannot get rid of it. I have been to therapy. I have made so much progress. I see the whole thing for what it was now. But no matter how far I come, I just cannot get rid of the letter. It's the only physical proof I have that I didn't make it all up in my mind. So, when I stop believing my own story, I pull it out."

The thing I love most about women is they are wise, intuitive, and compassionate beings. Women care about knowing and being known, so they listen and recognize importance. When these women heard that I kept your letter as a reminder of our story, they saw something that I could not. They saw the way I had allowed your words to tell my story.

And so I have made the decision to reclaim my voice. I decided to use these words that you selected, whether carefully or recklessly, to tell the story as it appears to me. I have left nothing out. I started at the beginning, the real one, not the one you would have me believe. Because our story did not begin when I graduated or when I turned eighteen. Our story began with a wide-eyed ten-year-old girl and her twenty-four-year-old teacher. With each line of your letter, I shed light on those fragile years I spent looking to you as my leader.

I have titled this book using your words, *Thinking of You*, because the truth is, even though I would rather not, I am still thinking of you.

34
Thinking of You: The Letter

College—Year Two

Mary Beth,

In our world of instant communication I thought it would be nice to send you an old-fashioned card complete with real handwriting (okay, printing but beggars can't be choosers.) As our relationship, friendship, continues to grow, so does my joy. You have become a very special person to me and I am so glad you re-entered my life. Though this time in a very different capacity. I can't wait to see what God has in store for you, me, and us. I truly wish I was able to be closer to where you are, it would be nice to see you in person. You know the old adage: "Distance makes the heart grow fonder." I think there's truth to that if we let it sink in and let God do His stuff! Doesn't make it any easier though, does it?

I know that in this time of waiting I think of you daily and fondly. You have shown me how to treat a woman. Your heart is for and of the Lord and that makes me rejoice! I remember you once told me I was a man of God. Though you couldn't see, a tear came to my eye and even still my heart beams with gladness at the thought. Getting to know you and who you are as a child of God makes me want to be the person I am looking for. The first spark in my mind and heart was when I was able to share my "coming back" or Prodigal Son moment with you over Christmas break. I knew then that things were different between us and I had a lot to think about. I honestly didn't want that conversation to end. Beautiful thing is . . . it hasn't. I thank God for that. He has shown me so much through you.

I know you struggle with image issues and how others view you. I start this way to say that you are a radiant beauty and you shouldn't be ashamed of that. We can only control what we can control and that's not others, especially not their thoughts. Though my former comment is true, I believe your real beauty is inside and it shines through to the outside. You are seeking, you are hungry for the Lord → that is beauty. Put it all together and you beam. I am humbled by the fact that you have even thought of me as more than a friend. Be assured that wherever this path God has placed us on goes I will follow and I know you will too. Let us pour into each other and others and rejoice in the saving grace of Jesus. The debt He paid is beyond all!

I am so happy that Christ is first between you and I. That gives me such comfort and peace. We have talked about obstacles or road-blocks that might be in the way of us being anything other than "just friends." A good quote for that is "If God brings you to it, He will bring you through it." I am putting it in God's hands, He is so much better than I. In the meantime, I can't wait to see what He has in store for both of us. He is already working and that's incredible. I have to admit . . . July seems so far away. However I will say that I want more time to see you this time. Maybe some time to experience face to face interactions. What a novel concept?! Your heart and its contents mean the world to me as it has already poured into me and made me glad!

I hope this letter finds you well and in good spirits.

In Christ's (and my own) Love,

W

35
My William

"... the person I am looking for."

College—Year Two

As spring break approached during my sophomore year of college, I was less than excited. I had hoped to attend a trip with my church but had no means to finance the trip. I had added my name to a list of students hoping to receive the support needed to cover the cost of attendance. About a week before this break, I had lost hope and resigned to spend my break at my parents' house. That's when I received an invitation. A peer had raised more than enough support for her own attendance and pledged the extra money to cover me. I was endlessly grateful for the opportunity to be a part of what my church called "Beach Reach."

I attended a meeting on the Wednesday before the trip. About thirty students were packed into one of the smaller classrooms in the business building. I slid into a seat, intimidated by the social circles. None seemed to overlap with my own, and I was feeling out of place. In the corner, the football players were sprawled on top of the desks, as if they owned the place. In a sense, they did. As the leading staff member took his place at the front, the students got quiet. From the back, a tall boy with light freckles, dark hair, and the body of a defensive lineman shuffled through the desks to join the group of football players. I remember thinking it was odd that

I didn't recognize him. I also remember fixating on how large and handsome he was. "William's here, everyone!" someone yelled in the front, interrupting the staff member's welcome. He was embraced by several of his teammates before he propped himself casually against the wall.

The meeting continued with logistics for the trip. We were headed to Panama City Beach to spread the gospel to what we called the "Spring Breakers." We would drive the strip of nightclubs and offer rides to the drunk young adults we found there. Once they were trapped in our car, we would share the good news of Jesus Christ, as if that might become the single most important event of their life. The thought now makes me cringe. We split into gendered groups to discuss dress codes and potential challenges. The men were warned about lusting after the women in bikinis at the beach, while we were forbidden to show our stomachs. I made a mental note to purchase a one-piece.

On Friday, you and I spoke on the phone. I was packing while we spoke, preparing to leave the following morning. I told you all about my trip and you encouraged me. You said you were proud of me for choosing to use my free time for the Lord. I was predictably glad to receive your praise. You asked how I had been feeling since our conversation about "obstacles" in our relationship.

The truth was that I had been doing a lot of thinking. I thought about our future together and what it would mean to call you "boyfriend." I wondered whether you would visit me at college and found that I hated the idea of that. I imagined the conversation with my parents. I imagined the one with yours. A future with you, one where we pulled our relationship from hiding, was daunting and messy. I was overwhelmed by the choice. I worried we would never know peace together. I was dealing with the complexity of my devotion to you, the desire for my youth, and the deep need to please everyone around me.

I took a deep breath and spoke the truth, "I have felt the weight of our decisions since we talked last week." Although it was not a lie, this only scratched the surface. I did not tell you about how I worried you didn't want children like I did or that you would erase my time to be a young adult. After all, I was nineteen, and these complex, adult thoughts were unfamiliar to me. You were thirty-four, consequently in the thick of decisions I had no business being a part of. I loved you, but I wasn't sure if that was enough for me. I had started to desire happiness and ease, two things I was not sure you could give to me.

It was in a rare moment of prioritizing my own peace that I said, "I think I would like a week to clear my mind, and I cannot do that when we talk. If it's alright, maybe we don't talk while I am gone? I want to be able to trust my thoughts and . . . well, it's easy to get caught up in my feelings. Am I making sense at all?"

You were gracious, more so than I expected. "Of course. You are full of wisdom, Mary Beth Wilson." You chuckled. "I love learning from you. Anyway, enjoy your trip and stay safe. Is it okay if I check in to know you are safe?"

"Of course it is." I smiled.

The trip from Ohio to Florida is a long one. We embarked on our journey in a herd of rental vans. We left before the sun had risen and drove well into the night. It was around 10 p.m. when traffic appeared rapidly. We wondered out loud what had happened as we heard the sirens. I remember the dread watching the lights fly past us and the relief when we confirmed our caravan was safe. We noticed a car with its hazards stopped in the middle lane. An officer was directing traffic to split around an obstruction in the road. I looked out my window as we passed and saw a woman crumpled against the car. We could hear her wails through the door. A few feet farther, I saw a man's lifeless, bloodied body lying in the road. I shut my eyes against the sight, but it wasn't enough to keep the image from my mind. The car fell silent as we drove through the disaster.

The group decided to pull over and allow us a chance to breathe in the fresh night air. Everyone was rattled by the sight. I remember exiting the van in silence and watching as my peers fell into each other's arms. I wasn't particularly close with anyone on the trip. I felt suddenly alone and cold. I stood under the light of a street lamp attempting to shake the tragic images from my mind. I watched the group hugging and crying. I watched as the tall man with the broad shoulders, William I thought, put his hand on his friend's elbow and nodded in my direction. He turned and walked my way, stopping when he reached the light. I had examined him from a distance all day, as he joked and tossed a football during each of our stops, but this was the first time I saw him up close. He had a short, well-kept beard and his hair had a slight wave I hadn't noticed before. The light highlighted the freckles along his cheeks. Though he was a stranger to me, his soft, deep brown eyes inexplicably filled me with comfort.

"Hey," he said softly, "you okay?"

I was a little intimidated at this moment by the attractive college athlete who had for whatever reason decided to approach me. It did not compute, but those teddy eyes of his pulled the answer from me anyway. "A little shaken, but yeah, I think I am." I wiped at the tears that had fallen down my face.

"Can I hug you?" he asked, with an inspiring level of confidence.

I nodded, again wondering why this man was over here with me. Before I could overthink, he stepped in and wrapped me in his arms. He was big and strong, and I had never felt anything as secure as his embrace. My heart glowed and seemed to whisper to me, though I couldn't quite catch its words. We stayed like that, just holding one another for a long time. Long enough that my tears stained his shirt. He didn't seem to mind.

"I'm William, by the way," he said when he finally pulled away from me.

"I know," I returned, laughing a little at the awkwardness of this whole encounter. "I'm Mary Beth."

His eyes scrunched in a small smile. "I know."

I laughed at that and his smile grew. "Want to walk with me?"

We spent that evening walking as our fellow travelers collected themselves. Eventually we set off and I spent the rest of the drive assessing the glow in my chest. I wasn't sure what had just happened, but I knew I was grateful that it had.

The next morning, I woke up in my shared room at the beach. I silently padded past the other girls, still asleep in their beds, and down the stairs with my journal. I intended to spend the morning in prayer and reflection about you. I sank into a chair on the sand and started to write. As I did, a group of boys approached from behind. By their general noisiness and gruff voices, I could tell this was the group of football players. They strode past, jostling each other and laughing. The boy with the dark hair—William, I was sure now—gave me a quick smile as he passed.

They set themselves up in a circle and proceeded in what I believe was a workout but looked more like a competition, one that consisted of seemingly endless push-ups and planks. Every now and then, a pair would sprint along the shore while the others hollered behind them. Though they had started the morning with their shirts on, the fabric had started to cling to them, drenched in sweat. Many chose to ditch the shirts entirely. It was quite a sight to behold. I tried to avoid the drift of my eyes, but I found them lingering on all those exposed chests and biceps. There were so many muscles over there, glistening in sweat and sun. William was, to me, the most attractive of the group, and I flushed at the fantasies that had involuntarily started playing in my mind.

I tried to journal, but as I did my mind continued to press. *Look at the boy. He's my age. What would I do with a boy my age?*

The boy in my thoughts came over as the crew wrapped up their workout. His hair clung to his head in a sloppy pile. He attempted to dry his face with his shirt, which only accentuated the curve of his muscles. I forced myself to look away as I felt the heat in my own face. He sank down in the sand next to me.

"Hey," he said simply as he tousled his hair with his shirt. "Enjoying the beach?"

"I am. Did you have a good workout?" I teased.

"Oh, yeah. We aren't technically supposed to have the week off, so Nate told our coach he'd run a beach boot camp. You could join tomorrow if you wanted." He gave me a look that suggested this invitation was genuine.

The laugh that escaped was louder than I expected. "Oh no, I don't think I could do one push-up if I tried . . . but I may take a jog in the sand sometime."

He laughed and tossed his shirt into the sand. "Am I interrupting?" he asked, pointing to the open journal in my lap.

"I was just finishing up," I lied. I snapped the journal shut and turned to him. "It's too hot for me."

"So hot," he agreed.

"Well, are you going to cool off in the water or what?" I nodded out to the ocean where the other football players were jumping into the waves.

"Absolutely not," he shook his head furiously. "I don't mess with the ocean."

"Me either. I don't even feel great about being this close to it," I admitted with a dramatic shudder. "It's too dark and unknown and . . . fishy."

He jumped up and extended a hand to me. "Well then, let's put some distance between us and the fish."

We went for a walk together. We found a gift shop where we laughed over the absurd tokens for travelers. He found every pun in the shop infinitely hilarious, which I found wonderfully adorable. I learned that he was from Wisconsin and had just transferred from California because he wanted to play for a Division I school.

When I pretended to understand what that meant, he called my bluff. "You can admit you aren't a lover of football. I won't be offended."

"Would you be upset if I said I have never even attended a game at BG?" I asked.

"I'd be more offended if you lied to me." He smiled.

That evening we sat around the pool. Lights twinkled above, and if we were quiet enough we could hear the crashing of waves into the shore. I sat next to William again. We had spent the whole day finding excuses to be near each other. Our feet were dangling in the water as we discussed our degrees and possible plans for our lives. It was so comfortable, discussing the future with this boy. Nothing hinged on my answer, and I had nothing tied up in his decisions. It was just easy. Getting to know William felt like freedom, and I was forced to consider that I may never feel that way with you.

Someone interrupted us by thrusting a guitar into William's lap and announcing it was his turn to lead us in a song.

I gave him a curious look. "You play?"

In answer, he started to strum. His voice had me awestruck. This was the moment when music fed the spark that had been flickering in my chest, and I realized I had a lot to think about.

In the following days, I thought a lot about William. I thought a lot about you, too. I weighed the two against each other. The spark of attraction vs. the depth of devotion. I pictured my life with you. It was heavy with obstacles to overcome at each turn. I pictured a future with William. It was light, filled with firsts and the flutters of butterflies. I felt the conflict rising within me and resisted the discomfort as best I could.

At some point, late in the week, I caught the stomach bug. We were out on the streets, handing out cards to partygoers and calling our people to come offer a ride when we saw it was needed. I became suddenly cold, though my face was dripping with sweat. I ran to the grassy area beside the bar and collapsed to the ground, willing myself not to get sick out here on the streets. Though, in all honesty, I would not have stood out if I had. William was not in my group, but his van had stopped nearby for a passenger. I was mortified when he walked over, crouched down, and placed a gentle hand on my forehead.

"You okay? You don't look so good," he said. Those brown eyes filled with concern.

"That's rude," I tried to joke, but I was so weak my breath came out in a huff.

"Can you walk?" he asked, ignoring my attempt at sarcasm.

"I don't know." I felt shaky and cold again. I worried I might throw up if I tried to stand.

Before I could protest, he was carrying me to the van. He buckled me in and said something to the driver that I couldn't hear. I felt detached, as if I were floating my way through a fever dream. We pulled into the parking lot at our strip of condos and I meant to say something about how the night wasn't over yet and he shouldn't leave on my account, but I couldn't find my words.

William helped me from the car, and we staggered all the way up the stairs to the door of my room before realizing I didn't have a key. There were only two to share among the group and I was not given one. I started to cry from exhaustion. The night felt endless and all I wanted was to crawl into the dark room. William pulled me to him and muttered comfort in my ear. He used the end of his shirt to dry the sweat from my forehead. He thought for a moment before deciding to take me to his room. He laid me in his bed and left to get me some water. He returned with a cold water bottle and checked in on me to be sure I was at least conscious. "I am going to give you privacy, but I am staying right outside. Let me know if you need anything, okay?" I wasn't conscious enough to give more than a nod, but if I could speak I would have asked him to stay.

Luckily the sickness was over almost as quickly as it began. I spent the night in misery and the next day sleeping. At some point, William must have returned me to my own bed with a brand new water bottle.

This is how I learned that this strong, athletic boy was also kind and gentle. I tried to imagine you caring for me and felt immediately embarrassed at the thought. I wondered if I would ever feel truly comfortable with you.

It was not any sort of competition between the two of you. It wouldn't have been a fair one if it were. I loved you and I liked him. It was the paradox of my choices that forced me to acknowledge what I had hoped to suppress. Even at nineteen, I knew that you and I would never be an even match, which forced me to the realization that I might never be happy with you.

In case you didn't know, I married this boy, the one who was fair and kind. He charmed me with his wit, but I fell in love with his mind. We were married the moment we graduated and have spent the past seven years building the most incredible life. He is my best friend, father of my incredible children, and the one I trust to hold my entire soul. My relationship with him is more sacred than anything I experienced in the walls of the church. He is my equal in every way, and I have never once doubted that he sees me as such. I could not be prouder of the man I chose.

I used to say that William saved me because he came into my life at such an opportune time. However, the more accurate truth is that choosing him saved me. He was not a prince pulling me from danger, but rather a light, illuminating a path to safety. He reminded me that I held the agency to choose, and choosing him was the greatest decision of my life. I no longer believe in the God I once did. Still, I thank every possible force in the universe for showing me that boy my age. Though, sometimes I wish it had done so sooner.

36

The Last Goodbye

"I honestly didn't want that conversation to end. Beautiful thing is . . . it hasn't."

College—Year Two

I returned from my spring break trip to a quiet dorm. Classes were not set to start for a few days, and the majority of students would not return to campus until it was necessary. I left the lights off in my dorm, tossed my bag on the floor, and crawled into my bed. The ride home from Florida was less eventful than our journey there, which had left plenty of time for me to spiral into the depth of my own feelings. Once there, I had been forced to the realization that my next move would be both necessary and horrifying.

The flurry of new feelings that I had discovered in Florida now cowered behind the enormity of my feelings for you. Though I had known with certainty what needed to be done, I lacked the courage to do it on my own. The complexity of our relationship meant that seeking counsel about you was nearly impossible. My teenage friends did not relate to the nature of my feelings, and I knew better than to involve an adult who might call you out as the bad guy. You had known that I was set to return from my trip, and I knew you were waiting for my call. Eventually, I had to admit to myself that I was not capable of moving forward without support. I pulled up Nikki's contact in my phone and was relieved to find that she had returned from her spring break trip as well.

Campus was shut down due to the lack of student activity, so we had decided to walk to our favorite coffee shop downtown, Grounds for Thought. I think you would have loved that place. It was a small bookstore with a vintage aesthetic that smelled like cinnamon. Coffee was served in mismatched mugs and if you were lucky, a musician would be playing acoustic music quietly in the far corner.

Nikki and I ordered our coffees and curled up in our favorite little nook of the shop. I shared my experience in Panama City and gushed about the football player I had met. Then, with our legs curled into our chests and warm mugs wrapped in our hands, I explained the complexity of you. At some point my phone buzzed with a text from you, which I left unopened.

"I just don't know what to do, Nikki." The words fell alongside heavy tears. "I don't know how to tell him that I can't follow where he wants us to go without ruining our relationship. I cannot stand the thought that he could be mad at me or worse, that I won't ever speak to him again."

Nikki was always the fiercest of my friends. She was safe, but honest. She was exactly the one I needed in this moment. She listened quietly to my story, leaving space for me to finish before responding. Then, in an act so true to her nature, she gave me a long hug, pulled away and said, "You have been given an out, and you have to take it."

"What do you mean?" I asked, shakily.

She squeezed my hand. "You don't have to jump into a relationship with this boy you met, but you can use him as an excuse to leave. That might be easier than trying to explain everything you are feeling."

She was right, of course. Saying I met someone I liked who was closer in both proximity and age seemed like the easiest explanation for my sudden change of heart. At the time, I wanted to believe that was the only excuse. I did not have the words for the shadows I felt around you, and even if I found them, I don't think I could have shared them with you. Until now, that is.

Together, Nikki and I developed an exit strategy. I would call you and tell you that the Lord had spoken to me. I would tell you about how I met a boy who seemed interested in pursuing a relationship with me, and it had forced me to consider my own needs and desires for a relationship. I would emphasize that regardless of where things went with this boy, I had learned that a romantic relationship was not something I could have with you given our circumstances.

I returned to my dorm feeling marginally prepared to talk to you. Even so, my stomach sank with dread when I finally opened your text.

Did you make it home? Can I call you? It would be good to hear your voice, I've missed you.

I said a quick prayer to the God I once thought capable of providing the courage I needed and typed my response.

I'm back and would love to catch up. You can call any time.

Seven dreadful minutes passed as I waited for your call. I paced my room and resisted the urge to toss my phone out the window and hide under my blankets. When you finally called it took four deep breaths for me to answer with a weak, "Hey."

"You're back," you said, with a hint of pain in your voice. "I had a tough week while you were gone."

This threw me off, and I paused to recollect my thoughts. I had been prepared to tell you about my trip and the decisions I had made while I was away. I had not prepared for you to be hurting.

"I'm sorry to hear that your week was so bad. What happened?" I managed.

You took a breath and for whatever reason determined I was capable of carrying the weight of the confession you were about to throw at me. (I was not.)

"I had to have a bit of a come-to-Jesus with myself. I tried to handle it alone, but I couldn't. I wanted to respect your wishes for space, but I really could have used your friendship."

"It's okay, you know you could have told me. Anyway, I'm here now. What is it?" In a moment I was once more pulled under this power you held over me, the one you had carefully constructed over the most formative years of my life. In hindsight, I don't think this timely confession of yours was an accident.

What you confessed in your next breath haunts me to this day. I have analyzed it from every angle and tried to conjure a thousand excuses for you. I have defended you to my therapists and excluded this piece in nearly every version of this story. Even my first attempt at putting this story on paper had minced your confession. The urge to protect you is still so strong. Unfortunately for you, I am determined to continue with the truth.

"I know that you know a bit about my marriage. There is more to that story. I told you I never felt intimacy with my wife, and that was often hard for me to handle. I am a person who craves intimacy. I don't remember how or when it started, but I have struggled with an addiction to porn. I use that word, addiction, because even when I can quit for a time, I always seem to fall back into that sin. It really bothered her, my ex-wife. Trying to stop for her is how I realized it had become a problem. Quitting did not come easily, so I started lying about it. I think my dishonesty played a role in the growth of the divide between us. I think that made it worse. I made it worse." You paused, but I did not fill the silence. Instead, I sat in a hushed shock. "I'm sorry, you must be so disgusted with me . . . " You trailed off and I could hear the sniffle of a cry through the phone.

Disappointment rang through my body as I realized that I would never be capable of walking away from you. Your brokenness had set off that instinctive need to protect you. Before I could stop myself, I began to speak.

"No, of course I do not think you are disgusting. I do not think any less of you at all. In fact, I think that it took a lot of courage for you to admit that to me, and I am grateful that you trust me enough to talk to me about it." I had been taught well to handle the confessions of men, though I was hit with a wave of nausea as I spoke this reassurance.

I felt the familiar weight of a battle I was too inexperienced to understand and the illusion that you were closing the gap between us with this act of vulnerability. Looking back, I realize this was no accident. Whether or not you would admit to it, you used this story to pull me back. Perhaps you felt me pulling back when I had asked for space and decided to use the power of your suffering to put me back where you liked me. With one small confession, I was back where the rush of power recharged you and made you feel bold and strong again.

I felt my own power evaporate as I listened in silence. You explained your battle with what you identified as addiction. You reiterated your beliefs on sex and intimacy, as if we hadn't already discussed them at length. As someone who had given my sexuality over to the church, I saw no issue with your need to confess, though I did wonder why you were confessing to me. Ultimately though, it started to make sense. After all, I had been taught that, as a woman, I was responsible for the sexual purity of men. Once again, I was a perfect victim. Once again, I am struggling to call this coincidence.

When the conversation ended, we hung up and promised to talk again soon. I buried my face in my pillow and cried. I felt every emotion from relief to sadness. Hot, angry tears spilled as I thought about the way our relationship would never recover from this. I was so angry with myself for missing my opportunity to leave, yet somehow also relieved to have stayed. The paradox of feelings was dizzying. I lacked the ability to explain my emotions at the time, but I know now that what I was experiencing was the result of our power imbalance.

I stayed in my bed with my phone in my hand, paralyzed by my own feelings. Whether I stayed like this for minutes or hours, I cannot recall. I felt a rush of feelings, but with each passing moment the anger grew bigger than the rest. I was so angry with myself for missing my opportunity to prioritize my own peace and angry with you for stealing my chance to do it.

I remember feeling the buzz of an incoming phone call and seeing your name again. I recall some inexplicable force propelling me to accept the call. I answered and prepared to listen to another nugget of advice your pastor had given or maybe even a lecture about the Lord's thoughts on porn. You were likely worried that you had colored my own sexuality by showing the dark side of yours. This is what I had come to expect from men in the church.

Instead, you apologized. "Hey, I'm sorry. I am so sorry. I dumped this on you and did not even take the time to ask about your trip. Please, tell me about your trip."

And just like that, there it was. My chance. I saw it like the closing light of the escape path in a movie. You know the scene where the hero is running from a dark cave as the rocks close in and then dives through the tiny hole left just before the final rock falls? This felt a lot like that. In a moment I saw the light and knew that if I could let my words out before my own thoughts caved in on me, maybe I would make this right. So, without thinking, I blurted the words I had rehearsed a thousand times in the past few hours. "It was great, but there is something I need to say. I met someone on this trip. I think he likes me and I think I like him too. He is my age and he is here and . . . well, I think I might want to pursue a relationship with him." I gasped, realizing I had not stopped for air.

I felt the desire to take it all back immediately. My thoughts twisted in a rushed attempt to make it right, but it was too late. I had done it. It was not eloquent or full of the complexity of my feelings, but it was enough.

You were calm and surprised me with the simplicity of your response. "When you said you wanted space, I thought that might be the case."

"I'm so sorry," was all I could say.

"No need to apologize, kid." Though you remained calm, I felt a coldness in your tone when you asked, "So, what's his name?"

I had no idea why you would ask me such a question and I dreaded giving you the answer. "I don't want to say . . . "

"Why? Do I know him?"

"No," I laughed uncomfortably, though I did not find any of this funny. "It's just . . . his name is William."

Now you laughed. The sound of it plagues my memories. "That's funny. Oh, man. God is funny. I deserve that."

Your reaction shocked me. "What do you mean?"

"Nothing, kid, nothing. Good luck with William. Good night."

Before I could respond, the line went dead. You had hung up.

I did not realize the gravity of it at the time, but this was the last time I heard your voice. Ten years ago, you laughed at me and then you vanished.

37
Sorry

"I think of you daily."

I am sitting at a cafe, hands wrapped around a cup of tea. I am leaning forward, chatting with my husband. He smiles at me and I feel safe. Until I see you. I feel as if the floor is falling from beneath me. I have to grab the table to remain steady when you walk by, your wife and baby trailing behind. You sit at a table directly in front of me, and I try to focus through your laughter. Suddenly, your hand is on my shoulder. You ask me if I would come with you. You are so close, I can feel your breath against my ear. My husband nods in a silent expression of good luck. I can almost hear him promising to come rescue me shortly. I follow you as you climb the staircase and lead me to a quiet, private space. We enter a small loft-like space above the shop. We are the only two in this room. You face me and take my hands in yours. You apologize to me. You say that your missteps with me have haunted you and you have been longing for a chance to make it right. I tell you that you could never make it right. You apologize again, this time through tears. I am tempted to forgive you, but I am reminded of the pain you caused. I shake my head and notice my own tears are hot on my cheeks. You step closer and wipe a tear away with your hand. You whisper this time, a simple "I'm sorry."

I wake myself up with the light sob that escapes my sleep. I'm sorry too, but for what, I'm not sure.

38
Uncovering the Truth

"Doesn't make it any easier though, does it?"

When you vanished from my life, I was forced to move forward without closure. It is strange how this has become more difficult over the years. I have heard it said that time heals all wounds, and yet the passage of time only caused this wound to fester. Ten years later, I think I am beginning to understand.

In order to allow myself to heal, I have had to admit that I had been choosing to believe in lies and half-truths. Frankly, I have done this because it was less painful than accepting the truth. Uncovering this truth was surprisingly simple. The difficulty came in accepting it. For every lie I let go of, I am forced to reckon with the facts. Once discovered, these facts drained the color of my childhood and projected the images of my memories in gray. Now, I repaint them in a new palette, one that is vibrant and lovely, as well as dark and haunting.

I once believed that you favored me because I was special. The truth is, I don't think I was ever chosen by you. I think this happened because I was driven and talented. I also gave you my attention readily. I used to feel guilty about this. Now, I understand that it is ordinary for children to desire the attention and favor of their authority figures. It is logical to believe that they will not abuse that position.

I once believed that I needed a man of God to lead me in a relationship. I believed it so fully that I looked to a grown man who I trusted to teach me. The teachings of my church became toxic for me when they made me believe that I, as a woman, held no agency. The truth is that I never needed a man or even a God. I am whole and fully capable as I am. I learn this every day as my husband and I lean on each other. He trusts me and we make decisions together. There is no leader. There is no follower. We are simply partners.

You told me that God led you to me. I believed you. I did not so easily dismiss this lie. It wasn't until I left the church that I realized the way this simple phrase has been used to excuse the behaviors of so many. What I have learned is that the church preys on the broken. It offered you wholeness in exchange for obedience. This so-called "obedience" allowed you to dismiss culpability for your choices because you were simply "following" a path laid for you. You stumbled into the church seeking connection, as many do, and you found me. I was prepared by the church to become the perfect victim, as most women are. You were taught that God's will does not fit into the expectations of the world. Together, we had set of excuses we needed to carry on with something that should have never been considered in the first place.

I once believed that you needed me. Allowing me to become someone you relied on was perhaps the worst of your transgressions. You needed a friend, and I was not in a position to be that for you. The truth is that I needed a friend too. In this regard, I do believe we both pushed the line for our own benefit. I do not tell this story to absolve myself of any guilt. I know that I was walking this path alongside you. However, now that I am closer to the age that you were at the time, I have the ability to forgive myself for acting my age.

I had started to believe that we had a romantic connection. I cannot speak to your side, but for my part I can say that I did have a genuine connection with you. We are, or were, very alike. You and

I experienced the world through music and we enjoyed sharing that experience. Our humors were similar, and at one time, our beliefs and priorities for life were seemingly aligned. I craved connection with a like-minded individual, and you were starved for it. Somewhere in my desire and in your actions, I forgot my place. The truth remains that the power dynamic between us made such a connection impossible. I merely attempted to suspend my disbelief.

I used to say that you were my best friend in high school. I wish you had the boundaries to make this belief impossible. You were my teacher. You made mentorship look like friendship. I do not think that is inherently bad. I have had plenty of mentors who have done so too. However, I no longer believe that teachers should be friends with their students. I hope you have learned this lesson as well.

The most difficult lie for me to let go of is believing that I am to blame for idealizing a relationship with my teacher. I had the fantasies of a teenage girl, this is true. I enjoyed every bit of your attention and came to crave more of it throughout the years. I drank up each drop of praise from you. However, while I am in some ways responsible, I am not at fault here. I may have pushed to maintain my connection with you, but you were the adult. It was quite literally your responsibility to both place and enforce the boundaries. Students have crushes on their teachers. This is a fact of life. It is the job of the teacher to discourage this. You cannot say you did not notice mine. I know better now. You leaned into this when you should have stepped back.

You and many other adults in my life made me believe that I was mature for my age.

I have come to resent this. While children may be more responsible than their peers, maturity is a holistic measure. I may have put work before play, followed every rule, and paid attention to things many neglect, but I also covered my walls in posters of the Jonas Brothers, threw fits when things didn't go my way, and exercised very little control over my feelings. When others said I was mature for my age, it made me believe that my developmentally appropriate behaviors were immature. So I tried to grow up too fast. I became convinced I would never bond with someone my age because of this.

Consider this my demand to stop saying this to children. Instead, let's encourage age-appropriate behavior and discourage preying on youth.

As I take on the laborious task of recovering the truth, I can admit that you were not as special as I once thought. As it turns out, your presence in my life was not the reason for my success. I have grown as a singer with the guidance of vocal teachers, music directors, and my peers. I have made friends and found love that encourages my independence and equity. The space you held in my life was important, and you betrayed me. The truth, I am finding, is complicated and unsettling, but it is also freeing.

39
Unsettled

"Be assured that wherever this path God has placed us on goes I will follow and I know you will too."

The end of our story was as abrupt as it was final. After we last spoke, you never resurfaced. At least, not in any tangible way. I struggled to end our story there, considering the enormity of its consequences. Over the past ten years, I have not heard from you. This does not mean that I have been entirely unaware of your presence, because I am aware. Painfully so, in fact.

In the years following you, I have had the common experience of discovering the humanity of my parents. These individuals that had once been idealized to the point of perfection have been recategorized as plainly and tragically human. Though often doing their best, they have never been immune to mistakes. For some, this is a jarring thought. For me, I find comfort in this. This is especially true now that I am a mother myself. Learning that I am not alone, that my parents are constantly learning from mistakes and adjusting their path accordingly, was a grounding experience.

I suspect it is normal to experience this with mentors as well. I have had a few important mentors in my life, though none quite like you. Confronting your humanity has been a difficult, confusing experience.

As a child, I put you on the highest pedestal. You spent ten years teaching at our little school. I always believed that you did this out of charity, that you were overqualified and perhaps underwhelmed by the opportunities and talent at our small school. I believed that instead of seeking more for yourself, you chose to give us more than anyone else could. I once modeled the teacher I wanted to become after you and your devotion to your students. In an email you sent me my sophomore year of college, you once wrote: "I never looked at teaching as winning competitions (obviously, we never did) or growing numbers. I looked and saw only people that I loved. Who they are is very important to me. We engage in music together, connect! It is not one-sided. I have cried during performances because the connection was so strong. Students have taught me many things."

When I first read this, I felt the swell of love and respect for who you were as a teacher and a man. I knew I had not imagined the glassy eyes that met my own while we performed together. I was always acutely aware of the way my peers never felt what we did, and I was angry for you. For all you had poured into us, for the emotions that we had shared, I thought you deserved the reciprocation I had given to you. I thought my peers were immature and ungrateful. I wanted you to know that I was different.

I once believed that what I saw in the raw emotions you chose to share with me was authenticity. I believed I was discovering your humanity. Instead I was developing a false perception. I once thought to question your honesty was betrayal. Now, I think the betrayal may have been yours from the start.

After your divorce, you moved away. This became the first of many long-distance moves. You moved to a place you had once idealized. I am sure you were hoping the clean slate would bring you peace. You were an unsettled spirit in search of something that I cannot name. First, you thought that you found it with the Christian God. You obsessed over the idea of Him. Your need for belonging and control was so strong that you chose to adopt an entire religion, for a time. You also chose to set your sights on a nineteen-year-old girl who was also lost in her own desire for stability and belonging. The key difference being that she was a child, where you were fully grown.

When we spoke, you expressed a desire to leave teaching. You were burnt out, exhausted from years of putting the needs of students before your own. You thought God saw something bigger for you, so you applied to seminary. You talked about the monks and expressed your desire to live as they do. What became of these endeavors is no longer my place to know. You cut me out before they had come to fruition. I wonder when this dream of yours was lost.

Since we last spoke, I have thought of you often. I began wondering, then worrying, that we might meet again. We had remained "friends" on social media, leaving me access to the few updates that you would post. First, I saw that you had, unsurprisingly, quit teaching. However, instead of becoming a pastor as you had told me, you obtained a license to become a barber. *That's odd*, I had thought, though I did not find it entirely shocking. I knew you needed that break from teaching and recalled the care you put into your own hair. *Maybe he will be happy now*, I thought, wistfully. Even then, I just wanted to be assured of your happiness.

About a year after I married my William, another update showed on my feed. You were also married. I am not embarrassed to admit that I opened those photos and read about your rustic wedding in the woods. Her name is similar to my own. "Strange coincidence," I thought. It rattled me a bit, to acknowledge the similarities in the names of our spouses. When I was younger, I would have wondered if this was some kind of sign. That perhaps you and I were twin flames. It was possible we had been connected in our lives before this one and were separated only by circumstance. That girl would have seen this as assurance that we were. That girl grew up and she knows better. *It does not mean anything*, I have reminded myself, each time I saw her name on your page.

Three years ago, I had started unpacking the trauma of our relationship in therapy. I was advised that the next step in healing required space. I opened my phone and deleted you from my Facebook page. The following day, when I scrolled to your page and hovered over the button to add you back as my friend, I forced myself instead to hit the block button. Blocking you was the only way for me to get the space I needed to uncover the truth of our relationship. For years, I took deep breaths and began the difficult work of believing that I had been a victim, that I had been your victim.

Two years ago, I went on a yoga retreat with my mom. We stayed in a cabin in the mountains of Georgia in late October and spent our time reading, doing yoga, and meditating in the stunning landscape. I was twenty weeks pregnant with my second son and in desperate need of the rest that came with that trip. One night, I sat curled up against my mother next to a crackling fire, a warm bowl of lentil soup in my lap. My mom's friend, Nancy, the one who sang with us in church, was there too. Together, we chatted about some of my peers and where they were now. Some had moved far away, others stayed close. Many were married and a few had become parents like I had. Then, Miss Nancy asked if I had heard from you.

"I have not," I shared, choosing to speak in small truths and leaving the rest unsaid.

"Oh," she seemed surprised. "He actually reached out to me just a few weeks ago. Did you know he is moving back?"

My stomach dropped and my breathing came in shallow gasps. I felt at once nauseated and thrilled in a way I cannot quite explain. I managed to ask only, "Back?"

"Believe it or not, yes. He is fully returning. He is going to be back in his old classroom and everything. What are the odds?" Nancy spoke without knowledge of the weight with which her news fell onto me.

What began as shock turned to a red, pulsing rage. It had been nearly a decade since you vanished from my life, and you had never once reached out to me to make things right. Instead, you had decided to come back to my home, a place where my family still lives, with a silent return. As if nothing had happened, as if you had no reason to hide, as if you expected me to let it happen without exposing you.

For years, I had seen your silence as the sound of your regret. In this moment, it felt more like indifference.

When I returned to my bed that night, I searched for more information on your movements. As I am sure you are aware, a quick search can tell you a lot about a person. I learned that you had lived in three states since we last spoke, with your return making four moves. You had taught at a few schools, but never stayed longer than a year. Between these teaching jobs, you had taken on many roles, including barber, podcast host, and retail worker to name a few. You were unsettled, that much was clear.

As healed as I was at this point, I was shaken by this new development. I had resigned to never see you again. I had accepted this as a sort of closure. I had felt comfortable sharing my story with others, knowing it was unlikely you would be touched by the consequences. Suddenly, there was a chance that I would see you again—one that felt big when I considered the size of our hometown and even larger when I learned you had moved to the town next to the one I lived and taught in back then.

That summer, I found the board minutes for my alma mater and read that William Davis had been approved by the board for hire into the position of choral director for middle school and high school, as well as director for the theater department. The following spring, I pulled up the theater website for my hometown, and found that you were directing the high school production of *Shrek the Musical*, a show that I was also directing at the high school in the neighboring town. *Not a sign*, I would remind myself daily. I felt plagued by your presence and often wished I would just run into you at the grocery or at the bar. I wanted to get past what I was sure was an inevitable reunion.

Last year, I received an unexpected notification on my social media page. William Davis had requested to be my friend. I laughed in shock. At first, I found humor in the idea of you feeling comfortable sending me this request. Then, I wondered why. What did you want now? What purpose did you have for trying to add me? Curiosity drove me to accept and I waited. I waited to see if this had finally been an attempt from you to apologize for your mistakes. I waited to see if you wanted to confront me for sharing my story and dreaded the idea that I may have to deal with your anger. Instead, I was met with more silence.

I explored your page and learned that you have a daughter who appears to be the same age as my oldest son. You are still married, but no longer teaching. Once again, you have left your job. I am not privy to your reasoning, but I speculate that it did not bring you the joy it once had. I think you are still seeking something that you have never found. I think you are still unsettled, even now.

According to my notifications, you watch my posts, though you are careful not to interact. Again, I wonder why.

Ten years ago, when you disappeared from my life, I confessed the entire thing to my mom. Through tears of disappointment, I told her about the things you had told me and the careful, difficult decision I had made. My mother held me as I spoke. When I tell my story, I am often asked, "What did your parents think?" The truth is that my parents protected me by keeping their thoughts hidden. If they had expressed concern, I would have run to you, which is a fact they knew well. I think my mom knew in this moment that my feelings were tender and that I was years from the rage I would eventually access. So, instead, she told me a gentle truth. "He is lost, Mary Beth, and you have escaped the tiresome path of loving someone who is unsettled."

My mother was right, and I think that truth remains even now. You are a transient soul, and I am glad to have left you to your wandering all those years ago.

40
For Good

"He has shown me so much through you."

As I contemplate my goal for telling this story, I find it important to continue to approach you with honesty. I want to be fair, even if our circumstances were not. I do not do this for you but for me, as I learn to cope with the reality of the present. I once thought that losing you meant losing all of my best memories and greatest accomplishments from my teenage years. For many years, I thought it had all been reduced to nothing by the decisions you made when I was nineteen. Then, I was forced to consider that my best memories were calculated attempts to groom and manipulate me. Now, I see that the mistakes you made in your brokenness do not entirely negate the positivity that you once brought to my life.

I wrote about honor choir in 2012 and how you encouraged me to audition and ate lunch with me when I was all alone. Auditioning for strangers was really scary for me at seventeen, but because you encouraged me to be brave I found that my hard work had given me the opportunity to sing with the best of the region. I gained confidence in myself as a singer and learned how to cooperate and sing with a new group and a new director. Later, when I went to college, this courage is the reason I was able to audition for the Women's Chorus. That was one of the greatest experiences of my life, and it provided me with chances to sing with professional orchestras and perform for diverse groups. I am thankful that you encouraged me to push myself outside of my comfort zone and still worked to make sure that it was a comfortable space for me.

I reflected on the preferential treatment I may have received surrounding our trip to Disney World and the burden of knowing your secrets while we were there. While the years of favor culminated in an inappropriate devotion to you that hung heavy on this trip, I also had so much fun exploring the parks and laughing my way through downpours and tornado warnings with my friends. Most of all, singing the solo "On My Own" was a once-in-a-lifetime experience. Whatever your motivation, I am grateful for the role you played in making all of this happen for me.

I recalled times when you listened to my worries and encouraged me through the wild roller coaster of emotions that is high school. You taught me to speak my mind, though I wouldn't fully accomplish this for many years. You helped me understand that the thoughts of others did not define my worth as a human. I learned a lot about life as I watched you navigate it yourself, for better or worse. Your authenticity and vulnerability, though problematic at times, shaped the person that I am today.

Reframing my past has been an important piece of my story. Much of the work to do this has been done in the pages of this retelling of our story. I have taken on the meticulous task of peeling your transgressions away from my youth and am left with something raw and tender. As I heal, I notice that the good and the bad have to exist together.

A few years ago, I joined a choir for the first time since college. The director was a woman and the difference was shocking to me. I did not realize the pressure I had been carrying until I made the active choice to let it go. I enjoyed making music with that group, and when I rehearsed, I did it for myself. There was no one to impress, no attention to seek. I sat in a group of adults who loved to sing and were choosing to use their precious free time to do so. It was simple and it was beautiful. I became close to that director, and I made sure to thank her for creating such a safe space for me to reclaim my love for choral music. I don't think she understood just how much I meant it at the time, but I am endlessly grateful to her for reminding me that singing in a choir was good for me.

A few years ago, the private voice teacher you had recommended to me, Mr. Black, reached out to me with an opportunity. The junior high school where he worked was looking for a codirector to help with their production of *Seussical Jr.* I was terrified at first, but I missed the theater, so I took a chance. I met one of my best friends and together we have created a safe space for kids to shine. We now direct both the high school and junior high musicals each year. Each year I am astonished that you did the things you did with me. I see the vulnerability of youth and the importance of holding space for them. I redeem my story by ensuring these kids never have one to tell. It is important work and it is good.

I have even made my way back into performance. There was a period in my life when I found myself overwhelmed by anxiety each time I sang. As I started uncovering the truth about our relationship, I started to doubt myself and my worth as a singer. I wondered if I was ever talented or if the solos and roles I had earned were merely chances for you to earn my trust. The insecurity was prevalent when I auditioned for a community theater show and found myself in the ensemble, which I had never experienced as your student. In this new role I learned when to sit back and watch my castmates shine. I learned to work collaboratively with others and made true, lasting friendships on stage. I met friends who are musicians and we make music together, and it is art. It is not emotional, traumatic, or heavy. It is light, fun, and free. It is good.

I started telling my story, and I found that others connected. I have been able to help others find the words for what happened to them and the courage to use their own voices. This is perhaps the most significant. What happened between us was objectively bad. However, I get to be a voice to teach others about grooming, boundaries, and spiritual manipulation, so that they might be able to avoid or recognize the things I had no knowledge of when they happened to me.

Inspired by the words of *Wicked*, I cannot say that I have been changed for the better. But, because of you I have been changed for good. I am forever changed. I am choosing to make it good.

41

On My Own (Part 5)

"Put it all together and you beam."

In the spring of 2024, I sat at set construction for a show I was directing. This time, I was the director. I was sitting cross-legged on the stage with an iced coffee in one hand and a hot glue gun in the other. We had been blasting show tunes and belting alongside the teenagers to shows like *Beetlejuice* and *Mean Girls*. I was having fun until the playlist shifted into a familiar, dreamy melody. My stomach turned as the music triggered a trove of terrible memories and feelings. Instead of belting out what was once my favorite show tune of all time, I set my coffee down and walked away. Before I knew it, my feet had carried me as far as the outside doors. I left the building and felt the chill of the March air fill my lungs as I grounded myself to my new reality. I reminded myself that I was safe. I stayed out there until I was sure the song had ended.

Trauma is a fascinating beast. Sometimes, it is a consistent little nudge, other times it fully stops me in my tracks. I have had to work really hard to take back the things that you stole from me. I have persisted through the anxiety that comes with these triggers, and every day I'm learning to face them.

No matter how much effort I put into redeeming my story, this song is something I cannot seem to take back. I often fear I can't reclaim something that was never truly mine. After all, you gave it to me that day in your classroom. Over those four years, my connection to you tied itself to this song in a knot that I thought would never be undone. Perhaps one day I will be able to belt this song with no thought of you, but I have resigned myself to knowing it is okay if I don't. I allow myself the grace to let things go, even if it feels unfair. Sometimes, that's the best we can do.

On my twenty-ninth birthday, my best friend, Hannah, presented me with a ticket to *Les Misérables.* She approached it with the gentleness and care of someone who understands the power of triggers, while knowing me deeply enough to understand how badly I wanted to attend.

"I know you may not be ready, but I will be there with you. We shouldn't let him keep this from you anymore," she had said.

I felt the burning of tears as I said, "I think I am ready, but only if you are there."

A few months later, we sat in the theater. The music, the characters, and the power of their story took my breath away, as it always has. I was reminded of the time I saw this show with my grandpa on one side and mom on the other. I realized you were nowhere to be found in that memory. I remembered the time I went to the movie theater with my dad, excited to see my favorite musical on the big screen, featuring Samantha Barks as Eponine. Again, you were not there. I recalled all of this while I made a new memory, there with my best friend.

The sweeping melody began to play and I felt myself tense with worry. I braced for the feelings that might come. The woman alone on stage began to sing a melody that is tragic and beautiful, and something incredible happened. I was so taken by the story and the moment, I forgot to think of you. My friend laid her head on my shoulder, and I forgot why I had been so afraid. I did cry, but those were the tears of a woman who loves this show, this friend, and this life she has built.

It turns out I can love this song, and I can do that without thinking of you.

Epilogue

Dear Mr. Davis,

I have finally found the name to call you, after all, this is who you always were to me. These are the words I leave with you. Whether you carry them forever or dismiss them immediately is no longer my concern.

The salty, bitter truth has been swallowed. The truth is that you never needed me to tell you this story. You know this story as well as I do. As much as I willed myself to be the author, it was you who crafted this narrative. I was a character in a plot created by your choices. As a teacher, you had the control. As a man, you had the agency. As an adult, you had the power.

And so it was written. We met when I was ten and you were twenty-four. By the time I was sixteen, we shared a level of intimacy that had been elevated with favor and secrecy. When I was nineteen you wrote to me, professing a desire to capitalize on the intimacy you had crafted. You were thirty-four. Three months later, you vanished.

Whether you felt shame or anger about this once felt consequential to me. I have believed that your excuse might help me understand how I should feel. Now, I know better. No excuse can absolve you of this, and whether you accept the shame or not, it will follow you forever. This is no longer my burden to carry for you.

This is my freedom. Despite how I feel about it, our story is already written. It is permanent. I cannot erase what was done to me, just as you cannot erase what you have done. Instead, we are both left to continue our lives in the epilogue. The space most often reserved for glimpses into happily ever afters are also the pages of reckoning, the pages of acceptance, healing, rage, and the entire spectrum of emotions in the aftermath. You have the freedom to choose whether you accept the role you played in my story or whether you continue your life in ignorance, just as I have the freedom to share my story.

I do not share my story to punish you, though at times the thought has been alluring. Instead, I share this story to teach the lessons that I have learned myself, that grooming can look like mentorship, a person can be both a good teacher and a predator, a child can be mature and still have a right to her youth, emotional abuse is still abuse, and stories are meant to be told.

~~Thinking of you,~~

With my final thoughts,

Mary Beth

About the Author

Mary Beth Runnoe was born and raised in Ohio. She received her degree in early childhood education from Bowling Green State University and spent the first few years of her professional career teaching. Mary Beth is a proud wife and mother of two wonderful boys. She has always found herself entranced by the power of story-telling, which has led her to a role as a stage director for her local school district. She is driven by a passion to embolden others to share their stories in the hope that doing so can inspire awareness, understanding, and connection.

About the Publisher

The Sager Group was founded in 1984. In 2012 it was chartered as a multimedia content brand, with the intent of empowering those who create art—an umbrella beneath which makers can pursue, and profit from, their craft directly, without gatekeepers. TSG publishes books; ministers to artists and provides modest grants; and produces documentary, feature, and commercial films. By harnessing the means of production, The Sager Group helps artists help themselves. For more information, please see TheSagerGroup.net.

More Books From The Sager Group

Miss Havilland: A Novel by Gay Daly

The Orphan's Daughter: A Novel by Jan Cherubin

Lifeboat No. 8: Surviving the Titanic by Elizabeth Kaye

Into the River of Angels: A Novel by George R. Wolfe

Who She Was: My Search for My Mother's Life
by Samuel G. Freedman

The Stories We Tell: Classic True Tales
by America's Greatest Women Journalists

New Stories We Tell: True Tales by America's New
Generation of Great Women Journalists

Newswomen: Twenty-five Years of Front-Page Journalism

The Someone You're Not: True Stories of Sports, Celebrity,
Politics & Pornography by Mike Sager

What Makes Sammy Jr. Run?: Classic Celebrity Journalism Volume 1 (1960s
and 1970s) edited by Alex Belth

Our Washington, DC: America's Hometown in Transition
edited by Susan Sheehan

The Dreyfus Collection: A Novel by Estelle Rubin Brager

See our entire library at TheSagerGroup.net

Artifex Te Adiuva

Printed in Dunstable, United Kingdom

67160814R00133